NATIONAL TEACHER EXAMINATION SERIES

THIS IS YOUR **PASSBOOK**® FOR ...

EDUCATIONAL TECHNOLOGY SPECIALIST

NLC®

NATIONAL LEARNING CORPORATION®

passbooks.com

PASSBOOK® SERIES

THE *PASSBOOK® SERIES* has been created to prepare applicants and candidates for the ultimate academic battlefield – the examination room.

At some time in our lives, each and every one of us may be required to take an examination – for validation, matriculation, admission, qualification, registration, certification, or licensure.

Based on the assumption that every applicant or candidate has met the basic formal educational standards, has taken the required number of courses, and read the necessary texts, the *PASSBOOK® SERIES* furnishes the one special preparation which may assure passing with confidence, instead of failing with insecurity. Examination questions – together with answers – are furnished as the basic vehicle for study so that the mysteries of the examination and its compounding difficulties may be eliminated or diminished by a sure method.

This book is meant to help you pass your examination provided that you qualify and are serious in your objective.

The entire field is reviewed through the huge store of content information which is succinctly presented through a provocative and challenging approach – the question-and-answer method.

A climate of success is established by furnishing the correct answers at the end of each test.

You soon learn to recognize types of questions, forms of questions, and patterns of questioning. You may even begin to anticipate expected outcomes.

You perceive that many questions are repeated or adapted so that you can gain acute insights, which may enable you to score many sure points.

You learn how to confront new questions, or types of questions, and to attack them confidently and work out the correct answers.

You note objectives and emphases, and recognize pitfalls and dangers, so that you may make positive educational adjustments.

Moreover, you are kept fully informed in relation to new concepts, methods, practices, and directions in the field.

You discover that you arre actually taking the examination all the time: you are preparing for the examination by "taking" an examination, not by reading extraneous and/or supererogatory textbooks.

In short, this PASSBOOK®, used directedly, should be an important factor in helping you to pass your test.

NATIONAL TEACHER / PRAXIS EXAMINATIONS (NTE)

INTRODUCTION

I. WHAT ARE THE PRAXIS EXAMINATIONS?

The Praxis Series Examinations comprise standardized tests that measure the academic achievement and proficiency of teaching applicants. Developed and administered by the Educational Testing Service (ETS), these exams evaluate the ability and knowledge of college seniors completing teacher education programs and advanced candidates who have received additional professional training in specific fields.

State departments of education and local school systems in this country that do not administer their own examinations for teaching positions may require teaching applicants to submit scores on the National Teacher Praxis Examination Series. These professional assessments of beginning teachers are designed to provide objective measurements of the knowledge, skills and abilities required in the teaching profession. These test results are then used for certifying teachers as initial, qualifying, validating, statutory, incremental, promotional and/or supervisory.

Additionally, many colleges use the Praxis Examinations in their teacher education programs at graduate and undergraduate levels, to provide student guidance and allow self-assessment by individual students. The Praxis tests have also been used as comprehensive examinations for undergraduate students and as qualifying exams for graduate students.

Three groups of tests at three different levels of assessment – Praxis I, II and III – constitute the Praxis Examinations. Praxis I measures basic academic skills, Praxis II measures general and subject-specific knowledge and teaching skills, and Praxis III assesses the practical skills demonstrated by the teaching applicant in a required classroom performance.

Praxis I exams are offered in both paper-and-pencil and computer-based formats in nationwide testing centers. Praxis II exams are given in paper-and-pencil format, while Praxis III is conducted in a direct classroom setting.

II. WHAT ARE THE PRAXIS I EXAMINATIONS?

Also described as Pre-Professional Skills Assessments (PPST), the Praxis I measures the candidate's proficiency in the basic academic skills of reading, writing and mathematics.

The PPST Reading and Mathematics test sections consist of 40 multiple-choice questions with 60 minutes of testing time in the paper-and-pencil format, with an additional 38 questions and an essay in the Writing test. The computerized PPST is made up of four separately timed sections – Reading, Mathematics, multiple-choice

Writing and Essay Writing. The testing session for the combined computer-based exam is 4-1/2 hours.

III. WHAT ARE THE PRAXIS II EXAMINATIONS?

Also categorized as Subject Assessments, the Praxis II examinations evaluate the candidate's knowledge of his or her professional area, as well as general and subject-specific teaching skills and knowledge. In addition to Subject Assessments, there are also Principles of Learning and Teaching Tests (PLT) and Teaching Foundations Tests.

The Subject Assessments (Specialty Area Tests) measure general and subject-specific skills and knowledge in a variety of teaching areas. These exams include both multiple-choice and constructed-response items. The PLT tests assess general pedagogical knowledge at four grade levels – Early Childhood, K-6, 5-9, and 7-12. These tests use a case-study approach and feature both kinds of test response items as well. Teaching Foundations Tests assess pedagogy in several areas – Multi-Subject (Elementary), English, Language Arts, Mathematics, Science, and Social Science.

A. What are the Core Battery Examinations?

Core Battery Examinations, still offered in some states, consist of a battery of three (3) discrete tests, which attempt to give a picture of the teacher-candidate's general ability and mental equipment. They are designed to measure the general educational background of college students, not to evaluate advanced preparation. The tests cover three categories: Professional Knowledge, General Knowledge, and Communication and Quantitative Skills. Professional Knowledge includes questions related to the social and cultural forces that influence curriculum and teaching, as well as questions related to general principles of learning and instruction. General Knowledge includes subtests on science and mathematics, social studies, literature and fine arts. Communication Skills measures listening, reading and written English expression and quantitative skills.

B. What are the Content Specialty Examinations?

The Content Specialty Examinations enable the candidate to demonstrate competence in a special field.

C. Which tests should you take?

Candidates for positions in the elementary school area usually take either Elementary Education or Early Childhood Education. Some school systems and colleges, however, require prospective elementary school teachers to take both.

Those who are candidates for secondary school positions customarily take the one Specialty Assessment covering their teaching specialty, although they are also sometimes asked to indicate another specialty – either in secondary education or even in elementary education.

Where school systems require teacher-candidates to take their own examinations in addition to the Praxis, these local exams are usually given at the same time. The school system to which application is made will notify the candidate whether such additional examination is to be given.

The only way to be sure which Praxis you should take is to get this information from the state department of education, the school system, the graduate school or the college to which you plan to have your scores sent.

D. Description of the examinations

The following are brief descriptions of the individual Core Battery and Content Specialty Examinations as drawn from the official bulletin of information for candidates:

CORE BATTERY EXAMINATIONS

The Core Battery Examinations are designed to appraise your general preparation for teaching. Tests are offered in (1) Professional Knowledge (including questions in Psychological Foundations of Education, Societal Foundations of Education, and Principles of Learning and Teaching), in (2) General Knowledge (including Social Studies, Literature and Fine Arts), and in (3) Communication Skills (Written English Expression). The General Knowledge and Professional Knowledge tests each include four 30-minute sections containing multiple-choice questions or problems. The test of Communication Skills consists of three 30-minute multiple-choice sections and a 30-minute essay. Course work beyond what is required by teacher preparation programs generally is not essential for the General Knowledge tests.

1. Professional Knowledge (Education)

The Professional Knowledge test is designed to provide an indication of the candidate's knowledge and understanding of professional education matters. It contains questions on general principles and methods of teaching, educational psychology and child development, guidance and personnel services, evaluation, principles of curriculum development, and significant research findings in education and related fields.

The test consists of four 30-minute sections, one of which is a pretest section. Each section contains 35 questions. The questions in the pretest section are administered solely for developmental purposes and do not contribute to examinees' scores.

This test assesses the examinee's understanding of the knowledge and skills that a beginning teacher uses in decision making, with emphasis on the context and process of teaching. Questions concerning the process of teaching assess knowledge of appropriate techniques or means of instructional planning, implementation and evaluation, as well as knowledge of what constitutes acceptable professional behavior. Questions concerning the context of teaching assess the examinee's ability to recognize constitutional rights of students and implications for classroom practice; the implications of state, federal and judicial policy; and forces outside the classroom that influence teachers and students. Some questions also assess the examinee's knowledge of activities and functions of professional organizations and of teachers' rights and responsibilities.

2. General Knowledge (Education)

The General Knowledge test assesses the examinee's knowledge and understanding of various disciplines and their interrelationships. The test consists of four separately timed 30-minute sections: Literature and Fine Arts, Mathematics, Science and Social Studies.

Social Studies, Literature and Fine Arts: In the modern classroom, the demands made upon the teacher's cultural background extend far beyond any one field of specialization. It is generally agreed that persons entrusted with the education of children need to have a broad perspective on significant factors in contemporary life. The Social Studies, Literature and Fine Arts test is designed to furnish an estimate of the breadth of the candidate's cultural background in these areas rather than mastery of any special subject.

The 30 questions in the Social Studies section of the test assess an understanding of (1) major United States historical and cultural events and movements, political institutions and political values; (2) prominent characteristics of societies and cultures; (3) relationships between culture and individuals; (4) economic concepts and processes; (5) and knowledge of geographical features and characteristics of human settlement and culture; and (6) social science methodologies, methodological tools and data resources.

The 35 questions in the Literature and Fine Arts section of the test are based on passages from literature, photographic reproductions of art works, film stills and photographs of theater or dance performances. The questions using these kinds of materials are designed to assess the examinee's skills in analysis and interpretation.

The *Science and Mathematics* test is designed to furnish an estimate of the candidate's knowledge of important concepts in the fields of science and mathematics, including contemporary developments in these areas.

The 30 questions in the Science section of the test are designed to measure knowledge and understanding of certain themes that are major areas of scientific interest and current concern. Questions selected emphasize important principles, theories, concepts and facts of science; applications of these theories and facts; and the methods of science. The science questions are based on important themes from the biological, physical and earth sciences.

The 25 questions in the Mathematics section of the test are intended to assess the examinee's cumulative knowledge of mathematics. Questions are selected from such topics as comparing and ordering numbers; estimation; interpreting graphs, charts and diagrams; use of ratio, proportion and percent; reading scales; measurement; interpreting formulas and other expressions written in symbols; logical reasoning; and recognition of more than one way to solve a problem.

3. Communication Skills (Written English Expression)

The Communication Skills test is designed to measure the two factors judged to be of particular significance for teachers: general verbal ability and skill in the correct use of the English language. The test contains questions on grammatical usage, punctuation, capitalization, spelling, sentence structure and organization, reading skills, and an essay. The test assesses the examinee's knowledge and skills in the areas of listening, reading and writing.

The Listening section consists of 40 questions that assess the examinee's ability to retain and interpret spoken messages. The questions and the information on which they are based are tape-recorded; they do not appear in the test book. Only the directions and answer choices are printed. Directions are also presented on the tape.

The section is divided into three parts, each with a different question format. In Part A, examinees listen to short statements or questions, then select either the best answer to a question or a sentence that is best supported by the statement. In Part B, examinees listen to short dialogues between two speakers, then answer multiple-choice questions. In Part C, examinees listen to several short talks, each followed by multiple-choice questions.

The Reading section consists of 30 multiple-choice questions that assess the examinee's ability to read for literal content and to analyze and evaluate prose selections. The reading material varies in difficulty and is drawn from a variety of subject areas and real-life situations. The section contains long passages of approximately 250 words, shorter passages of approximately 100 words, and short statements of fewer than 50 words.

The multiple-choice Writing section consists of 45 questions that assess the examinee's ability to use standard written English correctly and effectively and to select and order materials appropriately in sentences or short paragraphs. Examinees are not required to have knowledge of formal grammatical terminology, but rather are asked to detect errors, choose the best way to rewrite certain phrases or sentences, and evaluate strategies for developing ideas.

For the essay component of the Writing section, examinees are asked to write for 30 minutes on an assigned topic. The essays are scored holistically (that is, with a single score for overall quality). Scores are based on such things as the development of the central idea; evidence that the writer understands why the piece is being written and for whom; consistency of point of view; cohesiveness; strength and logic of supporting information; rhetorical force; appropriateness of diction and syntax; and correctness of mechanics and usage.

Guidance Counselor, Senior H.S.	NT-16c
Health Education	NT-38
Hebrew	NT-68
Home Economics Education (Family Consumer Science)	NT-12
Introduction to the Teaching of Reading	NT-39
Italian	NT-50
Latin	NT-18
Library	NT-17
Literacy	NT-70
Marketing and Distributive Education	NT-46
Mathematics	NT-6
Media Specialist – Library & Audio-Visual Services	NT-29
Men's Physical Education	NT-36
Music Education	NT-11
Office & Secretarial Technology	NT-58
Physical Education	NT-9
Physics and General Science	NT-7b
Psychology	NT-42
Reading Specialist	NT-30
Safety / Driver Education	NT-59
School Food Service Supervisor	NT-60
School Psychology	NT-40
School Social Worker	NT-65
Social Studies	NT-8
Sociology	NT-61
Spanish	NT-14
Special Education	NT-41
Speech and Language Pathology	NT-33
Speech Communication	NT-35
Teaching Emotionally Disturbed	NT-43
Teaching Health Conservation	NT-23
Teaching Hearing Handicapped	NT-28
Teaching Learning Disabled	NT-44
Teaching Orthopedically Handicapped	NT-25
Teaching Speech Handicapped	NT-26
Teaching Visually Handicapped	NT-27
Technology (Industrial Arts) Education	NT-5
Theatre	NT-69
Trades and Industrial Education	NT-22
U.S. History	NT-62
Visiting Teacher	NT-21
Vocational General Knowledge	NT-64
Women's Physical Education	NT-37
World Civilization	NT-63

IV. WHAT IS THE PRAXIS III EXAMINATION?

The Praxis III Examination evaluates the candidate's performance in the complex environment of the modern classroom, using the licensing criteria of the state in which the exam is administered.

As the practical section of the Praxis Series, the Praxis III Examination analyzes the candidate's ability to implement his/her ideas in the classroom. This exam includes a training program that utilizes the most recent materials and teaching techniques. The teacher's knowledge of the diverse requirements for different subjects is assessed, as is the candidate's ability to employ the teaching method that is particularly appropriate to the subject being taught.

Trained local observers constitute a qualified committee that examines the teaching applicant's understanding of the specific needs of individual students. Finally, the Praxis III evaluates the candidate's awareness of multi-cultural issues, an important criterion in today's classroom environment.

ABOUT THE EDUCATIONAL TECHNOLOGY SPECIALIST TEST

Foundations of Educational Computing and Technology
Professional Applications of Technology
Integrating Technology Into Education
Technology Leadership and Resource Management
Integrating Technology Into Education: Constructed-Response Assignment

---

The Educational Technology Specialist has the knowledge and skills necessary to teach effectively in public schools. The Educational Technology Specialist has a basic understanding of computer operations and concepts and is familiar with equity, ethics, and legal issues associated with the use of technology in education. The Educational Technology Specialist is knowledgeable about the professional applications of technology and is able to plan, implement, and assess concepts and skills relevant to educational computing and technology literacy for all students across the curriculum. The Educational Technology Specialist is able to apply technology-related research findings to the creation and maintenance of effective learning environments and knows how to develop and implement educational technology professional development programs to assist other educators in furthering their understanding of teaching and learning with technology. Finally, the Educational Technology Specialist understands issues related to facilities and resource management, and managing the change process in the educational environment.

SUBAREA I—FOUNDATIONS OF EDUCATIONAL COMPUTING AND TECHNOLOGY

0001   **Understand basic computer operations, concepts, and care.**

For example:

- demonstrating knowledge of various kinds of hardware, peripheral devices, and software found in the educational environment
- demonstrating knowledge of major operations systems associated with computing platforms found in the educational environment
- demonstrating knowledge of terminology related to computers and technology
- demonstrating knowledge of basic computing procedures (e.g., startup and shutdown sequences, network login procedures, routine system operating configurations)
- demonstrating knowledge of how to clean and maintain hardware, peripheral devices, and removable media
- demonstrating knowledge about virus scanning, opening and closing files, multitasking, saving files in multiple formats, and using shared files
- demonstrating knowledge of the installation of peripheral devices and related software

0002   Understand basic troubleshooting techniques for computer systems and related peripheral devices.

For example:

- recognizing appropriate methods for isolating problems and checking connections

- demonstrating knowledge of common problems with peripheral devices, Internet connections, and network use

- identifying strategies for troubleshooting various hardware and/or software configurations

- demonstrating knowledge of strategies for troubleshooting basic computer operating systems

- demonstrating knowledge of support resources and information for resolving technical problems

0003   Understand equity, ethics, and etiquette issues associated with the use of technology in education.

For example:

- demonstrating familiarity with equity, ethics, and etiquette issues

- demonstrating familiarity with issues of equity regarding computer use (e.g., students with special needs, students with limited English proficiency, students with different economic and social backgrounds)

- demonstrating knowledge of equity and ethics issues related to technology purchasing and policy decisions

- analyzing the historical development and important trends affecting the evolution of technology

0004   Understand legal, privacy, security, and safety issues associated with the use of technology in education.

For example:

- demonstrating knowledge of legal, privacy, security, and safety issues related to technology purchasing and policy decisions

- demonstrating knowledge of acceptable use policies for school-owned technology resources (e.g., publishing the names and photographs of minors, appropriate use of chat rooms and computer-mediated conversations)

- demonstrating knowledge of methods for protecting students from inappropriate information and interactions associated with the use of technology

- demonstrating an understanding of liability issues related to piracy, plagiarism, unauthorized access, and/or vandalism of software

- demonstrating knowledge of copyright laws related to the use of computers, software, and technology

- demonstrating knowledge of how to appropriately cite electronic sources

- demonstrating knowledge of health issues related to the use of computers (e.g., eyestrain, repetitive stress injuries)

SUBAREA II—PROFESSIONAL APPLICATIONS OF TECHNOLOGY

0005 **Understand the advanced features of technology-based productivity tools.**

For example:

- demonstrating familiarity with the advanced features of word-processing, desktop publishing, graphics programs, and utilities to develop products
- demonstrating knowledge of how to use spreadsheets for analyzing, organizing, and displaying numerical data
- demonstrating knowledge of how to design and manipulate databases and generate customized reports
- demonstrating knowledge of multimedia, hypermedia, and Web-based publishing
- demonstrating familiarity with teacher utility and classroom management tools
- demonstrating knowledge of how to identify, select, integrate, present, and publish video and digital images
- demonstrating familiarity with specific-purpose electronic devices (e.g., graphing calculators, language translators, scientific probeware)

0006 **Understand the features and uses of telecommunication, information access, and delivery systems.**

For example:

- demonstrating knowledge of how to use telecommunication tools for information access, retrieval, and sharing
- demonstrating familiarity with the use of electronic mail and Web browser applications
- demonstrating knowledge of advanced online search techniques for identifying and indexing information resources
- demonstrating knowledge of a variety of distance learning delivery systems (e.g., computer, audio, and video conferencing)

0007 **Understand the use of computers and other technologies in research, problem-solving, and product development.**

For example:

- demonstrating knowledge of principles of instructional design associated with the development of multimedia and hypermedia learning materials
- demonstrating knowledge of age- and grade-level appropriate computer-based technology tools for communicating concepts, conducting research, and solving problems for an intended audience and purpose
- demonstrating familiarity with strategies for creating and/or incorporating collaborative online workgroups into instruction to construct and share knowledge
- demonstrating knowledge of how to develop instructional units supported by technology that involve compiling, organizing, analyzing, and synthesizing information

0008   Understand methods and strategies for planning, delivering, and assessing concepts and skills relevant to educational computing and technology literacy across curricula.

For example:

- demonstrating knowledge of methods and strategies for teaching concepts and skills related to computers and associated technologies

- demonstrating knowledge of methods and strategies for teaching concepts and skills for applying productivity, information access, and delivery tools

- demonstrating knowledge of methods and strategies for teaching problem-solving skills using technology resources

- demonstrating knowledge of methods and strategies for evaluating the effectiveness of instructional units that integrate computers and technology

SUBAREA III—INTEGRATING TECHNOLOGY INTO EDUCATION

0009   Understand educational and technology-related research.

For example:

- applying principles and practices of educational research in educational technology

- demonstrating familiarity with major research findings and trends related to the use of technology in education to support the integration of technology in the educational environment

- demonstrating knowledge of learning and teaching theories and instructional design, and their relationship to the use of technology in the educational environment

- demonstrating knowledge of the social and historical foundations of the use of technology in education

- identifying research related to equity issues concerning access and use of computers and related technologies in education

0010   Understand principles of instructional design and product development.

For example:

- demonstrating knowledge of how to incorporate technology into curriculum development in alignment with state and national content standards

- demonstrating an understanding of criteria for evaluating instructional materials (e.g., alignment with content standards, student needs, ease of use, presentation features, authoring capability, ease of navigation, media integration, search strategies, instructional support)

- demonstrating knowledge of design principles for developing instructional materials (e.g., the design of screens, text, graphics, audio, and video)

- demonstrating familiarity with methods for the assessment and evaluation of instructional products

- demonstrating knowledge of how to apply instructional design principles for the development of substantive interactive multimedia computer-based instructional products

0011 Understand factors involved in creating and maintaining effective learning environments using technology.

For example:

- demonstrating knowledge of how to plan learning activities to include appropriate technology resources for students of diverse backgrounds and needs (e.g., prior knowledge, cultural and linguistic backgrounds)

- demonstrating an understanding of how to design, implement, and assess student learning activities that integrate computers and technology

- demonstrating knowledge of how to adapt or modify computer-based presentations for diverse student populations

- demonstrating familiarity with adaptive techniques and assistive devices for students

- demonstrating familiarity with methods for developing and adapting lessons to fit the classroom and the available technology (e.g., one versus multiple computers, networked versus stand-alone computers)

- demonstrating knowledge of how to manage computer technology activities along with other classroom activities

0012 Understand issues relating to software and hardware selection, installation, and maintenance in the educational environment.

For example:

- demonstrating an understanding of how to select effective technological resources appropriate to New York State Learning Standards, instructional objectives, and grade level

- identifying software used in classroom and administrative settings (e.g., productivity tools, information access and telecommunication tools, multimedia and hypermedia tools, school management tools, evaluation and portfolio tools, computer-based instruction)

- demonstrating knowledge of procedures for acquiring administrative and instructional software for various educational purposes

- demonstrating knowledge of evaluation criteria for software (e.g., support of content standards and instructional design, clarity of objectives, scope and scale, quantity of useful information, logical development and organization, appropriate reading and vocabulary levels, identification of bias or distortion of information), and identifying reliable sources of software evaluations

SUBAREA IV—TECHNOLOGY LEADERSHIP AND RESOURCE MANAGEMENT

0013 Understand methods and strategies for the use of computers and other technologies in developing and implementing instructional programs.

For example:

- demonstrating knowledge of strategic planning to facilitate curriculum development for teaching with computers and related technologies

- identifying national and state guidelines for integrating technology in the educational environment (e.g., National Education Technology Standards)

- evaluating the use of technology in the classroom and demonstrating knowledge of strategies for revising instruction when necessary

- demonstrating the ability to assume a leadership role in incorporating technology in the educational environment

- demonstrating familiarity with methods for promoting the awareness of emerging technologies

0014   Understand methods and strategies for designing, implementing, and evaluating educational technology professional development programs.

For example:

- demonstrating knowledge of professional organizations, groups, resources, and activities to support regular professional growth related to technology
- demonstrating knowledge of important factors to consider when designing educational technology professional development programs
- demonstrating knowledge of the steps necessary to design, implement, and evaluate educational technology professional development programs
- recognizing the importance of creating individualized professional development plans
- demonstrating knowledge of models for formal and informal educational technology professional development (e.g., providing in-classroom support, just-in-time training, job-embedded activities, peer-to-peer coaching, workshops)

0015   Understand issues related to facilities and resource management.

For example:

- demonstrating knowledge of budget planning and management procedures (e.g., prioritizing needs) related to educational computing and technology facilities and resources
- identifying funding sources available at local, state, and national levels and methods for developing grant proposals
- demonstrating knowledge of procedures (including ethical and legal issues) for resource acquisition and management of technology-based systems including hardware and software
- demonstrating knowledge of procedures for staffing, scheduling, and maintaining security with regard to the use of computers and technology in a variety of educational environments

0016   Understand issues relating to and strategies for managing the change process in the educational environment.

For example:

- demonstrating knowledge of change process issues in the educational environment
- demonstrating knowledge of procedures for evaluating school and district technology plans
- applying evaluation findings to recommend modifications in technology implementations
- demonstrating knowledge of issues relating to building collaborations, alliances, and partnerships involving educational technology initiatives
- demonstrating knowledge of effective group process and interpersonal skills

**SUBAREA V—INTEGRATING TECHNOLOGY INTO EDUCATION:
CONSTRUCTED-RESPONSE ASSIGNMENT**

The content to be addressed by the constructed-response assignment is described in Subarea III, Objectives 9–12.

HOW TO TAKE A TEST

You have studied long, hard and conscientiously.

With your official admission card in hand, and your heart pounding, you have been admitted to the examination room.

You note that there are several hundred other applicants in the examination room waiting to take the same test.

They all appear to be equally well prepared.

You know that nothing but your best effort will suffice. The "moment of truth" is at hand: you now have to demonstrate objectively, in writing, your knowledge of content and your understanding of subject matter.

You are fighting the most important battle of your life—to pass and/or score high on an examination which will determine your career and provide the economic basis for your livelihood.

What extra, special things should you know and should you do in taking the examination?

I. YOU MUST PASS AN EXAMINATION

A. WHAT EVERY CANDIDATE SHOULD KNOW
Examination applicants often ask us for help in preparing for the written test. What can I study in advance? What kinds of questions will be asked? How will the test be given? How will the papers be graded?

B. HOW ARE EXAMS DEVELOPED?
Examinations are carefully written by trained technicians who are specialists in the field known as "psychological measurement," in consultation with recognized authorities in the field of work that the test will cover. These experts recommend the subject matter areas or skills to be tested; only those knowledges or skills important to your success on the job are included. The most reliable books and source materials available are used as references. Together, the experts and technicians judge the difficulty level of the questions.

Test technicians know how to phrase questions so that the problem is clearly stated. Their ethics do not permit "trick" or "catch" questions. Questions may have been tried out on sample groups, or subjected to statistical analysis, to determine their usefulness.

Written tests are often used in combination with performance tests, ratings of training and experience, and oral interviews. All of these measures combine to form the best-known means of finding the right person for the right job.

II. HOW TO PASS THE WRITTEN TEST

A. BASIC STEPS

1) Study the announcement

How, then, can you know what subjects to study? Our best answer is: "Learn as much as possible about the class of positions for which you've applied." The exam will test the knowledge, skills and abilities needed to do the work.

Your most valuable source of information about the position you want is the official exam announcement. This announcement lists the training and experience qualifications. Check these standards and apply only if you come reasonably close to meeting them. Many jurisdictions preview the written test in the exam announcement by including a section called "Knowledge and Abilities Required," "Scope of the Examination," or some similar heading. Here you will find out specifically what fields will be tested.

2) Choose appropriate study materials

If the position for which you are applying is technical or advanced, you will read more advanced, specialized material. If you are already familiar with the basic principles of your field, elementary textbooks would waste your time. Concentrate on advanced textbooks and technical periodicals. Think through the concepts and review difficult problems in your field.

These are all general sources. You can get more ideas on your own initiative, following these leads. For example, training manuals and publications of the government agency which employs workers in your field can be useful, particularly for technical and professional positions. A letter or visit to the government department involved may result in more specific study suggestions, and certainly will provide you with a more definite idea of the exact nature of the position you are seeking.

3) Study this book!

III. KINDS OF TESTS

Tests are used for purposes other than measuring knowledge and ability to perform specified duties. For some positions, it is equally important to test ability to make adjustments to new situations or to profit from training. In others, basic mental abilities not dependent on information are essential. Questions which test these things may not appear as pertinent to the duties of the position as those which test for knowledge and information. Yet they are often highly important parts of a fair examination. For very general questions, it is almost impossible to help you direct your study efforts. What we can do is to point out some of the more common of these general abilities needed in public service positions and describe some typical questions.

1) General information

Broad, general information has been found useful for predicting job success in some kinds of work. This is tested in a variety of ways, from vocabulary lists to questions about current events. Basic background in some field of work, such as sociology or economics, may be sampled in a group of questions. Often these are principles which have become familiar to most persons through exposure rather than through formal training. It is difficult to advise you how to study for these questions; being alert to the world around you is our best suggestion.

2) Verbal ability

An example of an ability needed in many positions is verbal or language ability. Verbal ability is, in brief, the ability to use and understand words. Vocabulary and grammar tests are typical measures of this ability. Reading comprehension or paragraph interpretation questions are common in many kinds of civil service tests. You are given a paragraph of written material and asked to find its central meaning.

IV. KINDS OF QUESTIONS

1. Multiple-choice Questions

Most popular of the short-answer questions is the "multiple choice" or "best answer" question. It can be used, for example, to test for factual knowledge, ability to solve problems or judgment in meeting situations found at work.

A multiple-choice question is normally one of three types:
- It can begin with an incomplete statement followed by several possible endings. You are to find the one ending which *best* completes the statement, although some of the others may not be entirely wrong.
- It can also be a complete statement in the form of a question which is answered by choosing one of the statements listed.
- It can be in the form of a problem – again you select the best answer.

Here is an example of a multiple-choice question with a discussion which should give you some clues as to the method for choosing the right answer:

When an employee has a complaint about his assignment, the action which will *best* help him overcome his difficulty is to
    A. discuss his difficulty with his coworkers
    B. take the problem to the head of the organization
    C. take the problem to the person who gave him the assignment
    D. say nothing to anyone about his complaint

In answering this question, you should study each of the choices to find which is best. Consider choice "A" – Certainly an employee may discuss his complaint with fellow employees, but no change or improvement can result, and the complaint remains unresolved. Choice "B" is a poor choice since the head of the organization probably does not know what assignment you have been given, and taking your problem to him is known as "going over the head" of the supervisor. The supervisor, or person who made the assignment, is the person who can clarify it or correct any injustice. Choice "C" is, therefore, correct. To say nothing, as in choice "D," is unwise. Supervisors have and interest in knowing the problems employees are facing, and the employee is seeking a solution to his problem.

2. True/False

3. Matching Questions

Matching an answer from a column of choices within another column.

V. RECORDING YOUR ANSWERS

Computer terminals are used more and more today for many different kinds of exams.

For an examination with very few applicants, you may be told to record your answers in the test booklet itself. Separate answer sheets are much more common. If this separate answer sheet is to be scored by machine – and this is often the case – it is highly important that you mark your answers correctly in order to get credit.

VI. BEFORE THE TEST

YOUR PHYSICAL CONDITION IS IMPORTANT

If you are not well, you can't do your best work on tests. If you are half asleep, you can't do your best either. Here are some tips:

1) Get about the same amount of sleep you usually get. Don't stay up all night before the test, either partying or worrying—DON'T DO IT!
2) If you wear glasses, be sure to wear them when you go to take the test. This goes for hearing aids, too.
3) If you have any physical problems that may keep you from doing your best, be sure to tell the person giving the test. If you are sick or in poor health, you relay cannot do your best on any test. You can always come back and take the test some other time.

Common sense will help you find procedures to follow to get ready for an examination. Too many of us, however, overlook these sensible measures. Indeed, nervousness and fatigue have been found to be the most serious reasons why applicants fail to do their best on civil service tests. Here is a list of reminders:

- Begin your preparation early – Don't wait until the last minute to go scurrying around for books and materials or to find out what the position is all about.
- Prepare continuously – An hour a night for a week is better than an all-night cram session. This has been definitely established. What is more, a night a week for a month will return better dividends than crowding your study into a shorter period of time.
- Locate the place of the exam – You have been sent a notice telling you when and where to report for the examination. If the location is in a different town or otherwise unfamiliar to you, it would be well to inquire the best route and learn something about the building.
- Relax the night before the test – Allow your mind to rest. Do not study at all that night. Plan some mild recreation or diversion; then go to bed early and get a good night's sleep.
- Get up early enough to make a leisurely trip to the place for the test – This way unforeseen events, traffic snarls, unfamiliar buildings, etc. will not upset you.

- Dress comfortably – A written test is not a fashion show. You will be known by number and not by name, so wear something comfortable.
- Leave excess paraphernalia at home – Shopping bags and odd bundles will get in your way. You need bring only the items mentioned in the official notice you received; usually everything you need is provided. Do not bring reference books to the exam. They will only confuse those last minutes and be taken away from you when in the test room.
- Arrive somewhat ahead of time – If because of transportation schedules you must get there very early, bring a newspaper or magazine to take your mind off yourself while waiting.
- Locate the examination room – When you have found the proper room, you will be directed to the seat or part of the room where you will sit. Sometimes you are given a sheet of instructions to read while you are waiting. Do not fill out any forms until you are told to do so; just read them and be prepared.
- Relax and prepare to listen to the instructions
- If you have any physical problem that may keep you from doing your best, be sure to tell the test administrator. If you are sick or in poor health, you really cannot do your best on the exam. You can come back and take the test some other time.

VII. AT THE TEST

The day of the test is here and you have the test booklet in your hand. The temptation to get going is very strong. Caution! There is more to success than knowing the right answers. You must know how to identify your papers and understand variations in the type of short-answer question used in this particular examination. Follow these suggestions for maximum results from your efforts:

1) Cooperate with the monitor
The test administrator has a duty to create a situation in which you can be as much at ease as possible. He will give instructions, tell you when to begin, check to see that you are marking your answer sheet correctly, and so on. He is not there to guard you, although he will see that your competitors do not take unfair advantage. He wants to help you do your best.

2) Listen to all instructions
Don't jump the gun! Wait until you understand all directions. In most civil service tests you get more time than you need to answer the questions. So don't be in a hurry. Read each word of instructions until you clearly understand the meaning. Study the examples, listen to all announcements and follow directions. Ask questions if you do not understand what to do.

3) Identify your papers
Civil service exams are usually identified by number only. You will be assigned a number; you must not put your name on your test papers. Be sure to copy your number correctly. Since more than one exam may be given, copy your exact examination title.

4) Plan your time
Unless you are told that a test is a "speed" or "rate of work" test, speed itself is usually not important. Time enough to answer all the questions will be provided, but this

does not mean that you have all day. An overall time limit has been set. Divide the total time (in minutes) by the number of questions to determine the approximate time you have for each question.

5) Do not linger over difficult questions

If you come across a difficult question, mark it with a paper clip (useful to have along) and come back to it when you have been through the booklet. One caution if you do this – be sure to skip a number on your answer sheet as well. Check often to be sure that you have not lost your place and that you are marking in the row numbered the same as the question you are answering.

6) Read the questions

Be sure you know what the question asks! Many capable people are unsuccessful because they failed to *read* the questions correctly.

7) Answer all questions

Unless you have been instructed that a penalty will be deducted for incorrect answers, it is better to guess than to omit a question.

8) Speed tests

It is often better NOT to guess on speed tests. It has been found that on timed tests people are tempted to spend the last few seconds before time is called in marking answers at random – without even reading them – in the hope of picking up a few extra points. To discourage this practice, the instructions may warn you that your score will be "corrected" for guessing. That is, a penalty will be applied. The incorrect answers will be deducted from the correct ones, or some other penalty formula will be used.

9) Review your answers

If you finish before time is called, go back to the questions you guessed or omitted to give them further thought. Review other answers if you have time.

10) Return your test materials

If you are ready to leave before others have finished or time is called, take ALL your materials to the monitor and leave quietly. Never take any test material with you. The monitor can discover whose papers are not complete, and taking a test booklet may be grounds for disqualification.

VIII. EXAMINATION TECHNIQUES

1) Read the general instructions carefully. These are usually printed on the first page of the exam booklet. As a rule, these instructions refer to the timing of the examination; the fact that you should not start work until the signal and must stop work at a signal, etc. If there are any *special* instructions, such as a choice of questions to be answered, make sure that you note this instruction carefully.

2) When you are ready to start work on the examination, that is as soon as the signal has been given, read the instructions to each question booklet, underline any key words or phrases, such as *least*, *best*, *outline*, *describe*

and the like. In this way you will tend to answer as requested rather than discover on reviewing your paper that you *listed without describing*, that you selected the *worst* choice rather than the *best* choice, etc.

3) If the examination is of the objective or multiple-choice type – that is, each question will also give a series of possible answers: A, B, C or D, and you are called upon to select the best answer and write the letter next to that answer on your answer paper – it is advisable to start answering each question in turn. There may be anywhere from 50 to 100 such questions in the three or four hours allotted and you can see how much time would be taken if you read through all the questions before beginning to answer any. Furthermore, if you come across a question or group of questions which you know would be difficult to answer, it would undoubtedly affect your handling of all the other questions.

4) If the examination is of the essay type and contains but a few questions, it is a moot point as to whether you should read all the questions before starting to answer any one. Of course, if you are given a choice – say five out of seven and the like – then it is essential to read all the questions so you can eliminate the two that are most difficult. If, however, you are asked to answer all the questions, there may be danger in trying to answer the easiest one first because you may find that you will spend too much time on it. The best technique is to answer the first question, then proceed to the second, etc.

5) Time your answers. Before the exam begins, write down the time it started, then add the time allowed for the examination and write down the time it must be completed, then divide the time available somewhat as follows:
   - If 3-1/2 hours are allowed, that would be 210 minutes. If you have 80 objective-type questions, that would be an average of 2-1/2 minutes per question. Allow yourself no more than 2 minutes per question, or a total of 160 minutes, which will permit about 50 minutes to review.
   - If for the time allotment of 210 minutes there are 7 essay questions to answer, that would average about 30 minutes a question. Give yourself only 25 minutes per question so that you have about 35 minutes to review.

6) The most important instruction is to *read each question* and make sure you know what is wanted. The second most important instruction is to *time yourself properly* so that you answer every question. The third most important instruction is to *answer every question*. Guess if you have to but include something for each question. Remember that you will receive no credit for a blank and will probably receive some credit if you write something in answer to an essay question. If you guess a letter – say "B" for a multiple-choice question – you may have guessed right. If you leave a blank as an answer to a multiple-choice question, the examiners may respect your feelings but it will not add a point to your score. Some exams may penalize you for wrong answers, so in such cases *only*, you may not want to guess unless you have some basis for your answer.

7) Suggestions
   a. Objective-type questions
      1. Examine the question booklet for proper sequence of pages and questions
      2. Read all instructions carefully
      3. Skip any question which seems too difficult; return to it after all other questions have been answered
      4. Apportion your time properly; do not spend too much time on any single question or group of questions
      5. Note and underline key words – *all, most, fewest, least, best, worst, same, opposite,* etc.
      6. Pay particular attention to negatives
      7. Note unusual option, e.g., unduly long, short, complex, different or similar in content to the body of the question
      8. Observe the use of "hedging" words – *probably, may, most likely,* etc.
      9. Make sure that your answer is put next to the same number as the question
      10. Do not second-guess unless you have good reason to believe the second answer is definitely more correct
      11. Cross out original answer if you decide another answer is more accurate; do not erase until you are ready to hand your paper in
      12. Answer all questions; guess unless instructed otherwise
      13. Leave time for review

   b. Essay questions
      1. Read each question carefully
      2. Determine exactly what is wanted. Underline key words or phrases.
      3. Decide on outline or paragraph answer
      4. Include many different points and elements unless asked to develop any one or two points or elements
      5. Show impartiality by giving pros and cons unless directed to select one side only
      6. Make and write down any assumptions you find necessary to answer the questions
      7. Watch your English, grammar, punctuation and choice of words
      8. Time your answers; don't crowd material

8) Answering the essay question

Most essay questions can be answered by framing the specific response around several key words or ideas. Here are a few such key words or ideas:

M's: manpower, materials, methods, money, management
P's: purpose, program, policy, plan, procedure, practice, problems, pitfalls, personnel, public relations
   a. Six basic steps in handling problems:
      1. Preliminary plan and background development
      2. Collect information, data and facts
      3. Analyze and interpret information, data and facts
      4. Analyze and develop solutions as well as make recommendations

5. Prepare report and sell recommendations
6. Install recommendations and follow up effectiveness

b. Pitfalls to avoid
1. *Taking things for granted* – A statement of the situation does not necessarily imply that each of the elements is necessarily true; for example, a complaint may be invalid and biased so that all that can be taken for granted is that a complaint has been registered
2. *Considering only one side of a situation* – Wherever possible, indicate several alternatives and then point out the reasons you selected the best one
3. *Failing to indicate follow up* – Whenever your answer indicates action on your part, make certain that you will take proper follow-up action to see how successful your recommendations, procedures or actions turn out to be
4. *Taking too long in answering any single question* – Remember to time your answers properly

EXAMINATION SECTION

EXAMINATION SECTION
TEST 1

DIRECTIONS: Each question or incomplete statement is followed by several suggested answers or completions. Select the one that BEST answers the question or completes the statement. *PRINT THE LETTER OF THE CORRECT ANSWER IN THE SPACE AT THE RIGHT.*

1. In the computer lab, students are getting ready to print a report for your class. However, when they try to print, they find that the printer is not receiving any print commands, so what should you do?
   A. Call your principal so he can buy a new printer
   B. Purchase new ink cartridges and replace the old ones
   C. Reset the printer's properties
   D. Look at the computer's default printer settings

1._____

2. File compression software has led to which types of files being downloaded more often, resulting in greater risk to intellectual property rights?
   A. Smaller files such as e-mails and company memos
   B. Larger files such as movies, songs and software
   C. Smaller files like PowerPoint presentations with audio
   D. None of these are at risk from file-compressing software

2._____

3. Copyright laws dictate that a program can be legally copied on a personal computer if and only if it is
   A. for educational purposes
   B. purchased with a site license exception
   C. used to archive the software in case of maintenance/repair
   D. not sold to someone else by the original user

3._____

4. Which of the following would strengthen a technology director's role within a school district?
   A. Cooperating with teachers to help recognize and integrate appropriate technology resolutions
   B. Finding out the cost and benefits of integrating proposed technology
   C. Keeping current with technology improvements
   D. Instruct subordinates so they understand technology improvements

4._____

5. When looking at the total cost of owning programs that track student information, finance, curriculum and more, a technology director can
   A. identify all systems and their relative costs
   B. determine the pragmatism of purchasing and implementing a new technology
   C. find out the staff requirements and skill levels needed
   D. get an approximation of replacement cycles and costs

5._____

6. Your students are searching for a research topic in the library and they want
two of their terms to appear on the same page. Which BOOLEAN entry
would the librarian tell them to use in order to achieve this purpose?   6._____
   A. And
   B. Or
   C. In Addition
   D. Not

7. A touch screen is closely related to which of the following devices?   7._____
   A. Scanner
   B. Light pen
   C. Joystick
   D. Keyboard

8. Within a disk, blocks of data are written into _____ sector(s).   8._____
   A. one
   B. two
   C. three
   D. two or more

9. Student A and Student B are arguing online and Student A makes a racist   9._____
   comment about Student B. Since it was online, there is a record of what
   Student A said, so his school has proof to suspend him for his comments.
   What is the lesson about online etiquette that Student A could benefit from?
   A. Don't share your opinion because people will twist it to make you
      sound awful
   B. Always put a smiley face at the end of every text line so people will
      know you are joking
   C. Be careful what you say because it may be saved and could come
      back to haunt you
   D. Don't post racist comments online because that is illegal and could
      result in jail time

10. Which of the following situations does NOT need an online citation?   10._____
    A. Using information from an online article that you put in your own
       words
    B. Using an image from a website for your assignment
    C. Writing that Yahoo is a commonly used search engine
    D. You need to cite in every one of these situations

11. Which of the following is a common injury from too much computer usage?   11._____
    A. Posture-related injuries
    B. Depression
    C. Eyestrain
    D. Both A and C

12. Microsoft Windows is a(n)   12._____
    A. character user interface
    B. operating system
    C. operating environment
    D. none of these

13. A condition where a ping program sends tons and tons of packets to a server   13._____
    in an effort to overwhelm its ability to handle high amounts of traffic is called a
    A. ping storm
    B. pagejacking
    C. jam sync
    D. jumbogram

14. Which of the following is a method of verification used when you need to   14._____
    check for errors in data that has been transmitted on a communications link?
    A. BeOS
    B. Remailer
    C. Cyclic redundancy checking
    D. Traceroute

15. Which software development phase allows users to sample the product so   15._____
    developers can troubleshoot?
    A. Out of the box
    B. Lexical scoping
    C. Regression testing
    D. Beta test

16. The audio signal given out by a computer to announce the result of a short   16._____
    diagnostic testing sequence the computer performs when first powering up is
    called a
    A. birdie
    B. beep code
    C. click
    D. hiccup

17. Ethics on the Internet is known as   17._____
    A. nethics
    B. net-manners
    C. netiquette
    D. net ethical and moral behaviors

18. Jon finds himself in an ethical dilemma related to an e-mail correspondence   18._____
    he is having with another person. He comes to you to ask what he should do.
    You tell him to
    A. e-mail a college professor who teaches about ethical behaviors
    B. think about how he would act in a real face-to-face scenario and
       follow that lead
    C. talk to someone with more experience in these matters
    D. do whatever he feels like because he likely won't get caught

19. You are reviewing your colleague's e-mail to an educational journal and notice that he has signed it with a smiley face at the end. You tell him
    A. to erase the smiley face as it is too informal and inappropriate
    B. replace the smiley with something more clever or comical
    C. nothing; it's his responsibility to understand Internet etiquette
    D. nothing; a smiley face never hurt anyone

19._____

20. Which of the following things should you NEVER do in an online chat setting?
    A. Post your home address
    B. Post your picture
    C. Post your comments on an assignment
    D. Post a reply to someone else's comments that you disagree with

20._____

21. You are trying to convince your board of education to purchase "ergonomic" keyboards but one board member raises his hand and asks you to define ergonomics. What should you tell him?
    A. It ensures that your hardware will be reliable and won't break down
    B. It helps make sure there are no work accidents
    C. It is the latest in environmentally friendly green technology
    D. It is a scientific look into designing safe and comfortable equipment

21._____

22. Which of the following situations would NOT be considered a health and safety issue concerned with computers?
    A. Exposed wires running underneath desks and chairs
    B. A coffee pot plugged into nearby outlets and placed beside a group of computers
    C. Wires tied, labeled and fed directly to wall and ceiling outlets
    D. Overloaded electrical sockets

22._____

23. One of the administrative assistants at the district office complains of injuries due to repetitive strain. Which of the following computer-related activities likely caused the injury?
    A. Recording and uploading notes from meetings every day
    B. Clicking on advertisements that pop up from a personal e-mail account
    C. Typing for hours each day
    D. Both A and B

23._____

24. When the first Unix OS was in its development stage, it was written in _____ language.
    A. C
    B. assembly
    C. B
    D. none of these

24._____

4

25. You go to your local library to log onto your Facebook page and on the wall   25._____
next to the computer the following message is posted: "Lurk before you leap."
What do the librarians mean by this message to their patrons?
    A. Make sure to always be anonymous when on the Internet
    B. Lurking is always an acceptable method of approach on the Internet
    C. It is important to know everyone in your social media area before you
       jump into conversations, that way you can do so with names and
       important information
    D. None of the above

KEY (CORRECT ANSWERS)

1. D		11. D	
2. B		12. B	
3. C		13. A	
4. A		14. C	
5. A		15. D	
6. A		16. B	
7. B		17. C	
8. D		18. B	
9. C		19. A	
10. C		20. A	

21. D
22. C
23. C
24. B
25. C

TEST 2

DIRECTIONS: Each question or incomplete statement is followed by several suggested answers or completions. Select the one that BEST answers the question or completes the statement. *PRINT THE LETTER OF THE CORRECT ANSWER IN THE SPACE AT THE RIGHT.*

1. Of the following devices, which would not be classified as input?   1._____
   A. Printer
   B. Keyboard
   C. Optical character reader
   D. Joystick

2. Which input device should you use if you want to play a computer game?   2._____
   A. Mouse
   B. Touch screen
   C. Joystick
   D. Keyboard

3. A teacher notices that one of her students has failed to properly give credit for   3._____
   a persuasive phrase that the student took from another source. This failure
   to properly credit a source is best known as
   A. paraphrasing
   B. fair-use policy
   C. laziness
   D. plagiarism

4. Which of the following would NOT be a violation of computer copyright laws?   4._____
   A. A student accidently breaks your CD you were going to use for next
      class. You decide to make a copy of other important discs so this
      won't happen again.
   B. A geology teacher has more students and computers than software.
      He decides to burn several extra copies so that each student can work
      on their own computer.
   C. A student downloads a new film from the Internet and uses a clip from
      it for his project
   D. All are in violation of copyright laws

5. A signal that is used to synchronize transmission between two or more   5._____
   systems is referred to as
   A. preamble
   B. ringtone
   C. Synclink
   D. semaphore

6. In TCP/IP, the algorithm that makes it possible to recover data packets is   6._____
   A. fast retransmit and recovery
   B. concatenation
   C. talkback
   D. cache coherence

7. When you talk with students about the plagiarism, which of the following should you make clear is a potential consequence?
   A. Receiving a zero for the assignment
   B. Having their high school diploma suspended or revoked
   C. Legal issues with the original author of the plagiarized work
   D. Both A and C

7._____

8. A student is viewing her professor's lecture online and she wants to use the professor's notes in her essay. However, the professor did not share the source used for the lecture notes. What should the student do?
   A. Cite the professor's lecture as the source
   B. Search for that information on the Internet hoping to find the original source
   C. Use the information and don't worry about citing it
   D. Don't use the information; she should only use information when it has the source attached to it

8._____

9. Which of the following programs tailored to a business that costs more than a software suite?
   A. Graphics/Multimedia
   B. Custom
   C. Home
   D. Business

9._____

10. This type of application software is legally protected, but can be freely downloaded for a short trial period.
    A. Freeware
    B. Shareware
    C. Restricted Trial
    D. Open Source

10._____

11. The technology director of your district is worried that recently purchased software might be installed on more computers than the school district has licenses for. What should she do in order to avoid legal issues?
    A. Use a pass code
    B. Have someone from the company assist the installation
    C. Use product activation
    D. Use an encryption code

11._____

12. What is used as the interface between a computer user, his or her application software, and the computer hardware?
    A. System software
    B. Allusion software
    C. Application crossing
    D. Utilities program

12._____

13. Which of the following would NOT be categorized as system software?   13._____
    A. Windows Vista
    B. Mac Snow Leopard
    C. OS
    D. None of the above

14. A specific mixture of letters, numbers and special characters used to identify   14._____
    files is more simply known as file _____.
    A. record
    B. extension
    C. name
    D. query

15. If a student wants to type a letter, a memo or even create a Web page,   15._____
    which of the following should s/he use?
    A. Spreadsheet database
    B. Word processing software
    C. Presentation software
    D. Publishing software

16. A computer's operating system is tasked with performing which of the   16._____
    following functions?
    A. Detecting viruses
    B. Compressing data
    C. Defragging disks
    D. Managing memory

17. Your students are about to post in your English class blog online. Which of   17._____
    the following are reminders you should give them before they start posting?
    A. Be clear
    B. Be knowledgeable
    C. Be succinct
    D. All of the above

18. In a computer class, students are tasked with organizing files and folders on   18._____
    their own computers. Which of the following would best help them
    understand how to do this?
    A. Explain the importance of different file extensions
    B. Have students create folders and move different files into each one
    C. Show how files are physically stored versus when in the cloud
    D. Make students create files and store them to the cloud

19. A high school English teacher wants his students to learn about the
    relationship between writing and literacy. He has his students in small
    groups and they will eventually demonstrate their findings in front of the
    class. The teacher is not sure which of the following activities should be
    used. What would be the best option for him?
    A. Have students use Microsoft Excel to present their findings
    B. Have students find articles on the Internet and show them to the class
    C. Have students print off articles from an encyclopedia from CD-ROM
    D. Have students create a database from which they can draw analysis
        of statistics

    19._____

20. A technology director is in the process of gathering technology-integrated
    lessons for the district. Which of the following would be the MOST essential
    contemplations when creating curriculum to meet instructional goals?
    A. How interested the teachers are in technology
    B. How original the lessons are
    C. How adaptable the technology lessons are
    D. How talented teachers are with the technology

    20._____

21. Your class just finished a unit and you want to do a self-reflection piece to
    figure out just how well the unit taught students to research on the Internet.
    What activity would help you determine how effective this lesson was?
    A. Make your students engage in a formal debate about the best ways to
        find significant information on the Internet
    B. Have students look back through their Internet search history and
        compile a list of the websites they used
    C. Give a lengthy short-answer quiz on the practices of Internet research
    D. Individually conference with each student and have them explain the
        process through which they created their projects

    21._____

22. As technology director, you talk with teachers who constantly ask you for the
    latest versions of software for their classroom computers. How should you
    decide to upgrade to the newest available software?
    A. The simple desire to own the latest version is enough
    B. A cost-benefit analysis with benefits outweighing costs
    C. Analyzing how many users can be added to the newer version
    D. Analyzing how long the current software has been used

    22._____

23. Mr. Jones is attending a conference in which the presenter will speak about
    technology integration into lesson plans. Which of the following would help
    Mr. Jones the MOST in trying to integrate technology into his curriculum?
    A. The presenter asks the group ahead of time about their future units so
        everyone can work on specific ways to incorporate technology
    B. The presenter provides the group with a database of lesson plans
        that successfully use technology
    C. The presenter demonstrates the different kinds of programs and
        computers that are available for schools to purchase
    D. The conference organizers dispense a list of technology tools that the
        group might find handy

    23._____

24. Teachers coaching other teachers can be a great way to develop
    professionally in educational technology because it
    A. offers a way for principals to informally assess teachers' skill in using
       technology
    B. gives educators the ability to have experts train them one-to-one
       assistance that can be customized
    C. provides teachers with a technology support system based on
       whatever needs they might have
    D. creates a network of teachers who can provide each other with
       feedback and support in educational technology

    24._____

25. If a school district operates on a low technology budget, how should a
    technology director go about solving technology problems between the high
    school, middle school and elementary school?
    A. Request that a technology trained staff member be in each school's
       computer labs at all times
    B. Give all teachers the network access password so they can deal with
       the problems themselves
    C. Train a few tech savvy people how to solve simpler technology issues
       before calling in the tech director
    D. Make sure all teachers know the tech director's personal phone
       number so they can contact the tech director at all times

    25._____

KEY (CORRECT ANSWERS)

1. A		11. C	
2. C		12. A	
3. D		13. D	
4. D		14. C	
5. A		15. B	
6. A		16. D	
7. D		17. D	
8. A		18. B	
9. B		19. D	
10. B		20. C	

21. D
22. B
23. A
24. D
25. C

TEST 3

DIRECTIONS: Each question or incomplete statement is followed by several suggested answers or completions. Select the one that BEST answers the question or completes the statement. *PRINT THE LETTER OF THE CORRECT ANSWER IN THE SPACE AT THE RIGHT.*

1. A person who software is designed for is known as a(n)
   A. end user
   B. programmer
   C. customer
   D. professional

   1._____

2. How can multimedia help school-age children?
   A. It can replace direct reading from a textbook
   B. It can aid students in learning different and inspiring ways that will allow them to creatively express what they know
   C. It gives complete control of learning over to the students
   D. It will replace teachers in the future

   2._____

3. In order to keep track of your dietary habits over the course of a month, which of the following would be the BEST method of conducting this task?
   A. Spreadsheet
   B. Word processor
   C. Database
   D. Bar graph

   3._____

4. A teacher complains one day that he had his personal information stolen through a fake e-mail he responded to. Which of the following scams did the teacher fall victim to?
   A. Trolling
   B. Tracking
   C. Phishing
   D. Hacking

   4._____

5. An example of a peripheral device associated with technology would be all of the following EXCEPT
   A. keyboard
   B. external hard drive
   C. printer
   D. motherboard

   5._____

6. Which of the following would be the best method for educating students in how to use Microsoft Word?
   A. Coaching
   B. Lecture to them
   C. Scaffold lessons
   D. Have students recite information back to you

   6._____

7. Students are placed into groups for a project and they are required to assign themselves to roles they have never been in before. What is the major advantage of this strategy?

    7._____

    A. The teacher can identify student weaknesses in addition to strengths
    B. This provides a way for groups to cover for weaker group members
    C. Students will be forced to reinforce what they've learned by teaching their peers about roles they've held previously
    D. It allows the students to observe their own progress by juxtaposing with their peers

8. A teacher hands his Computers class a reflection assignment so he can improve his curriculum in the future. Students report that they loved the animation unit, but were bored with the unit on type. Using this information, what should the teacher do for future classes?

    8._____

    A. Nothing; these students don't get to determine what he teaches
    B. A project that has students design their own typefaces
    C. An extra animation project in which students create a character and put it in a scene
    D. An assignment that involves students animating the text of a sound recording

9. A Junior English class is about to begin a unit in which students will be required to participate in blogs. Before the unit begins, which of the following should the teacher make sure the students understand?

    9._____

    A. Online etiquette rules and regulations
    B. How to code in HTML
    C. The objectives and rules of the blog website
    D. None of the above

10. A small black-and-white photograph is put into a slideshow and appears to have lost image quality. When did this likely happen to the photo?

    10._____

    A. When it was enlarged to fit the slide
    B. When it was scanned into the computer
    C. When it was desaturated
    D. When it was inserted into the presentation

11. Which of the following best defines the "golden section"?

    11._____

    A. The text body that stays the same at the head of a document
    B. The middle 85% of a video image where all text should appear
    C. The cross section of fake lines that forces the viewer's eyes on a specific focal point
    D. A ratio that is used in art and design that shows a balanced, pleasing image

12. The process color model

    12._____

    A. creates a final tone through subtracting the brightness from white
    B. adds color to the process
    C. measures the color values in pixels
    D. is usually used in computer programs

13. Which of the following BEST defines computer-based training?   13._____
    A. Video games
    B. Training a computer to reject viruses
    C. A program that allows people to learn at their own pace with interactive software
    D. A virtual program that trains computers to perform routine tasks

14. Which of the following BEST illustrates the benefits of groupware?   14._____
    A. Group members can share programs, files and other resources
    B. Members can read e-mails from other group members
    C. Group members can feel like they belong somewhere
    D. It allows people to rely on others to do their work

15. Which historical event is thought to be primarily responsible for creating a new way of communicating, better known now as the Internet?   15._____
    A. The Cold War
    B. Vietnam War
    C. World War II
    D. Korean War

16. What is the best definition of the commonly known term "multimedia"?   16._____
    A. Images and text that moves throughout a website
    B. Integrating both still and moving images, text and sounds through computer technology
    C. Images and audio
    D. None of the above

17. A student in your online class keeps posting messages in all caps. When you e-mail her, you explain that she should   17._____
    A. keep using the all caps because it helps get her point across
    B. change to all lowercase letters because it doesn't feel as formal
    C. avoid using all caps because it conveys an aggressive tone and is not correct form
    D. none of the above

18. Why would someone use acronyms in an online setting?   18._____
    A. They are hilarious to look at
    B. They save time and keystrokes
    C. They make a user appear more literate
    D. Acronyms serve no real purpose

19. You want to hire a group of programmers whose job it is to expose security errors in new software so that your computer network will not fail. Which group should you hire?   19._____
    A. ERM Group
    B. Computer Emergency Response Team
    C. Microsoft Certified Systems Engineers
    D. Tiger team

20. What is the diagnostic test sequence called that a computer input/output system will run to find out if the keyboard, RAM, disc drives and other hardware are working properly?
    A. NetBIOS
    B. Safe mode
    C. Initial program load
    D. POST

    20._____

21. One of your colleagues is chatting with you through Google Hangouts and sends the message "BRB." What did that colleague just communicate with you?
    A. "Be right back"
    B. "Been really bad"
    C. "Be really brief"
    D. It's an inside joke

    21._____

22. The golden rule of online etiquette most closely resembles which of the following?
    A. Remember that you are speaking to another human being online
    B. Don't spam others unless you want to be spammed
    C. Never send viruses to your friends
    D. Be friendly and kind in online forums and through e-mails

    22._____

23. When a help desk personnel member describes a problem that is user-related and not software/hardware-related, they may refer to the problem as which of the following?
    A. Cuckoo egg
    B. Mouse potato
    C. PEBCAK
    D. Silicon cockroach

    23._____

24. The Clark County school board and superintendent decide it is time to start using social media for its school communications. What is the first step the technology committee should take in order to implement this project?
    A. Come up with a list of commonly used jargon and grammar style for people unfamiliar with social media
    B. Find out which employees already use social media
    C. Create personal accounts for employees on Twitter, Facebook and YouTube
    D. Look back at the district policies already in place with regards to teacher use of social media

    24._____

25. Teachers in your district constantly ask for professional development
regarding technology. Which of the following would best help them become
more adept with using technology in their classrooms?   25._____
    A. Giving teachers access to district technology resources and programs
       at all times
    B. Planning and developing staff skilled in online instruction and digital
       resources
    C. Creating specific learning modules for teachers and new staff
    D. Budgeting for staff members to be trained on district-owned resources

---

KEY (CORRECT ANSWERS)

1. A	11. D
2. B	12. B
3. A	13. C
4. C	14. A
5. D	15. A
6. A	16. B
7. C	17. C
8. D	18. B
9. C	19. D
10. A	20. D

21. A
22. A
23. C
24. D
25. B

TEST 4

DIRECTIONS: Each question or incomplete statement is followed by several suggested answers or completions. Select the one that BEST answers the question or completes the statement. *PRINT THE LETTER OF THE CORRECT ANSWER IN THE SPACE AT THE RIGHT.*

1. For a technology to be successfully implemented into a district, which of the following MUST happen?
   A. You must attain the support of the local community leaders
   B. You must acquire the support from knowledge-workers in advance
   C. You should perform a survey among students to find their readiness levels
   D. You must assuage parental concerns through proper channels

   1._____

2. What statistic would best show that students are getting equal access to technology resources within a district?
   A. Frequency of use as reported by students
   B. Number of devices per school
   C. Cost per student for technology
   D. Ratio of students to technology devices

   2._____

3. What is an important step a technology director should take to encourage teachers to use interactive technology in the classroom?
   A. Have teachers share examples of lessons that used interactive technology
   B. Create a curriculum plan that uses interactive technology and make teachers use it
   C. Look at the district technology plan and structure to make sure interactive technology can be enabled
   D. None of the above are important steps to take

   3._____

4. A 9th grade English teacher asks you to assist him in implementing the school's multimedia resources into a unit on *To Kill A Mockingbird*. How should you determine what technology the English teacher should use?
   A. How comfortable the teacher is with technology in the classroom
   B. The objectives outlined by the unit being presented
   C. The ability of the resources and presentation to entertain students
   D. How much time will be given in class to the unit

   4._____

5. A program that allows students to enter a combination of keys one key at a time instead of pressing multiple keys at the same time would most benefit which type of student?
   A. One who lacks self-assurance in using the keyboard
   B. A pupil who has the use of only one hand when entering data on a keyboard
   C. Someone who prefers to use the mouse rather than the keyboard for all tasks
   D. A student who uses an oversized keyboard because of visual impairment

   5._____

6. Mrs. Stephenson borrows a software program from Mr. Jones and installs it on her own computer to use for her classroom. Which of the following describes this situation?

    A. This was not a copyright violation because both teachers are from the same school

    B. This was not a copyright violation because the teachers made sure to never use the software at the same time

    C. This was a violation of copyright law because it is contrary to the licensing agreement

    D. This was only a copyright violation if Mr. Jones already made a backup copy of the software

6._____

7. In their upcoming unit, students will need to write and edit at a computer and meet with their teacher to conference on their work. Which question about learning is an important one for the teacher to consider before the unit starts?

    A. Will the type of word-processing software affect the quality of work for each student?

    B. Should students be allowed to publish their drafts unedited or should they have to wait until teacher review?

    C. Will students be allowed to use software tools to help them gain technological literacy?

    D. How will the amount of time spent on the computer influence social interaction between students in the classroom?

7._____

8. A firewall is put into place to protect the school from viruses and malware. Which of the following could compromise the firewall?

    A. A teacher allowing students to download and save files from the Web

    B. A teacher using a phone outlet to connect an external modem to their computer

    C. Leaving a computer connected to the Internet all day even though it is not used

    D. A teacher downloading a newer version of a free Web browser and installing it on classroom computers

8._____

9. Which of the following file extensions is MOST likely to contain a virus?

    A. .pdf

    B. .wav

    C. .jpg

    D. .exe

9._____

10. In a Windows OS, the Device Manager should be used for which of the following functions?

    A. Uninstalling Microsoft Word

    B. Changing the interrupt used by a modem

    C. Configuring a printer to use draft settings

    D. None of the above

10._____

11. A middle school technology committee has recently convened to find and   11._____
    implement the best software for improving students' keyboarding skills.
    What is the first step the committee should take?
    A. Create and agree upon the objectives that the keyboarding software
       should meet
    B. Create a needs assessment to determine the importance of
       keyboarding skills in each classroom
    C. Figure out which interface would be most appropriate for the users
    D. Download a trial version of the most popular software to evaluate

12. During a Distance Learning course, students complain that the video keeps   12._____
    halting and audio does not match with the video being displayed. What is
    the most likely factor for this technology glitch?
    A. Quality of the camera
    B. The display resolution
    C. Available bandwidth
    D. Computer compatibility between two locations

13. The school decides it wants to update its website so that it's available and   13._____
    accessible to visually impaired students. What is the best way to do this?
    A. Href tags for hyperlinks
    B. Image maps for navigating the site
    C. Alt tags to describe images
    D. Automatic refresh for all pages

14. In a jazz band class, the teacher records a rehearsal and finds that the audio   14._____
    playback is very poor. Which of the following indicates the BEST way to
    solve the problem?
    A. Rerecord the rehearsal through MIDI devices
    B. A surge in digital sampling rate
    C. Play the audio file through the computer's internal speaker
    D. Save the file in MP3 format and then play that file back

15. You create a teacher web page using web authoring software only to find   15._____
    out your page appears on the intranet, but not on the Internet. What
    concept are you missing from creating your web page?
    A. FTP protocol
    B. Bandwidth
    C. Firewall
    D. Web server

16. In order to create a successful technology systems plan, what is the MOST   16._____
    important thing to do?
    A. Generate a plan that figures in the total cost of ownership
    B. Create procedures for technology access by teachers and students
    C. Form a replacement schedule for old and faulty equipment
    D. None of the above

17. How many bits does a byte represent?   17._____
    A. 10
    B. 40
    C. 8
    D. 22

18. _____ is a standard code used to share information between a data   18._____
    processor and a communication system.
    A. ACM
    B. APL
    C. ANSI
    D. ASCII

19. Which of these would a mouse be connected to?   19._____
    A. LPT1 port
    B. LPT2 port
    C. the serial port
    D. none

20. According to the E-Rate, a discount schools receive for telecom services, 20._____
    schools can also get discounts on which of the following?
    A. Internal network wiring and connections
    B. Computers for school classrooms
    C. Professional development for staff members
    D. Educational software packages

21. Which of the following is NOT a type of computer network?   21._____
    A. LAN (Local)
    B. RAN (Remote)
    C. MAN (Metropolitan)
    D. PAN (Personal)

22. Which color coding of cable is used to connect two similar devices?   22._____
    A. Straight cable
    B. Cross over cable
    C. Serial cable
    D. All of the above

23. The protocol for specifying and controlling network traffic so that certain 23._____
    traffic types get precedence is known as
    A. differentiated services
    B. specification of a sequence of flow objects (sosofo)
    C. order of magnitude
    D. flow control

24. Mr. Jones is creating a unit on online communication and he is currently working on a lesson that features the differences between online and face-to-face communication. What is one absolutely critical difference that Mr. Jones should mention?

24._____

  A. A user's face cannot be seen, making it more difficult to show thoughts and intentions. This could lead to misunderstandings.
  B. You can use swear words in your real life, but it is not allowed online
  C. When speaking it is okay to be informal and use slang, but writing online should be polished and formal
  D. Online, it is way easier to get away with stuff. Go ahead and do whatever you want.

25. After opening an e-mail in your class, a student receives a message that states "Warning: your computer may be infected with a virus." What should he do?

25._____

  A. Make sure he forwards the e-mail to everyone else in the class
  B. Ignore the warning and continue checking his e-mail
  C. Call you over so you can go to a security website to check if there is a real virus attached to the computer
  D. Flag you down so you can tell the principal who will shut down the whole lab so the virus cannot spread

---

KEY (CORRECT ANSWERS)

1. B		11. A	
2. A		12. C	
3. C		13. C	
4. B		14. A	
5. B		15. D	
6. C		16. A	
7. D		17. C	
8. A		18. D	
9. D		19. D	
10. B		20. A	

21. B
22. B
23. A
24. A
25. C

EXAMINATION SECTION
TEST 1

DIRECTIONS: Each question or incomplete statement is followed by several suggested answers or completions. Select the one that BEST answers the question or completes the statement. *PRINT THE LETTER OF THE CORRECT ANSWER IN THE SPACE AT THE RIGHT.*

1. A computer's operating system is responsible for performing which of the following tasks?

    A. Virus detection
    B. Data compression
    C. Disk defragmentation
    D. Memory management

1.____

2. Which of the following is the first action to take when a printer is not receiving a print command?

    A. Check the computer's default printer settings
    B. Realign the printer's print heads
    C. Replace the printer's ink cartridges
    D. Reset the printer's printing properties

2.____

3. The emergence of file formats capable of compressing large amounts of information for easy transmission has most significantly contributed to which of the following technology-related concerns?

    A. Protection of intellectual property rights
    B. Prevention of computer hacking
    C. Protection of the right to free speech
    D. Prevention of software piracy

3.____

4. According to current software copyright laws, it is permissible to copy software designed for personal computers

    A. only for educational purposes
    B. only if the software was purchased with a multiple user or site license
    C. only for archival purposes
    D. only if the copies are not resold by the original purchaser

4.____

5.

Downloaded
clip art image

Web page with image
used as a button

5.____

A student is creating a Web page with a textured background and has downloaded a clip art image of an envelope to use as a button on the page. The clip art image file and a sketch of how the image is to appear on the Web page are shown above. In which of the following ways should the student modify the clip art image so that it appears on the Web page as illustrated?

    A. Crop the image so that anything outside of the white circle is deleted and save it as a JPEG file

    B. Set the background color outside the circle to be transparent and save the images as a GIF file

    C. Paste the envelope and surrounding circle into the textured background image and save it as a JPEG file

    D. Fill the space outside the circle with the background texture and save the image as a GIF file

6. Which of the following is the correct Boolean entry to use when searching for two terms appearing on the same page?   6.____

    A. AND   B. OR   C. PLUS   D. NOT

7. A middle school science teacher is preparing a lesson on the relationship between solar flare activity and global weather patterns. The students will work in groups to research the relationship and present their results to the class. Which of the following would be the most age-appropriate activity for the teacher to include in the lesson? Have the students   7.____

    A. use the graphing functions of a spreadsheet application to present their data

    B. access articles from an encyclopedia on CD-ROM

    C. use the Internet to access and analyze articles from online scientific journals

    D. create a database to perform statistical analyses on their data

8. Which of the following strategies will best help students understand how files and folders are organized in a computer?   8.____

    A. Explaining the significance of the various file name extensions

    B. Having students create folders and move files into them

    C. Explaining how files are physically stored on the hard drive

    D. Having students create files and save them to another storage medium

9.   9.____

Line	Former Teaching Behavior	Current Teaching Behavior
1	small-group instruction	whole-class instruction
2	cooperative social structures	competitive social structures
3	lecture and recitation	coaching
4	students learning different things	students learning the same thing

Which of the following lines correctly illustrates the shift in teaching behavior attributed to the increasing use of technology in the classroom?

    A. Line 1   B. Line 2   C. Line 3   D. Line 4

10. For a facilitator responsible for providing technology-integrated lessons for an entire district, the most important consideration to make when designing curriculum to meet instructional goals should be the   10.____

    A. teachers' interest levels in technology
    B. adaptability of lessons
    C. teachers' proficiency levels in technology
    D. originality of lessons

11. A teacher wants to assess the effectiveness of a unit that required the use of Internet research skills. Which of the following activities would be most useful for this purpose?   11.____

    A. Having a class debate about the best ways to locate relevant information on the Internet
    B. Reviewing the computers' browser histories to determine the Web sites accessed during the unit
    C. Giving students a quiz on Internet research techniques
    D. Having students explain the process through which they created their final products

12. A school's decision to upgrade to a new version of software should be based primarily upon   12.____

    A. the need to own the most recent software
    B. an analysis of added benefits versus the cost of the software
    C. the number of potential users of the new software
    D. how long the current software has been in use

13. An educational technology specialist is planning a workshop to help a group of social studies teachers learn ways in which to integrate technology into their lessons. For teachers to get the greatest benefit from this workshop, it would be most useful for the educational technology specialist to   13.____

    A. provide participants with a file of lesson plans that provide examples of cases where teachers have successfully incorporated technology into their teaching
    B. demonstrate the various kinds of hardware and software that are currently available at their school and describe their functions and capabilities
    C. distribute a list of various technological tools the participants might find useful
    D. survey the participants ahead of time about upcoming lessons so that they can work together on ways to incorporate technology into specific lesson plans

14. Peer-to-peer coaching is a valuable component of educational technology professional development programs primarily because it   14.____

    A. provides a reliable method for informal evaluation of teachers' ability to use educational technology
    B. offers teachers the chance to receive expert one-on-one training and assistance customized to their individual needs
    C. provides teachers with a source of technical expertise, support and advice based on their immediate needs
    D. helps establish a community of teachers who use educational technology and provide feedback and support for each other

15. A school district with limited resources has hired an educational technology specialist to work in the district's three small elementary schools. One of the specialist's responsibilities is to maintain the schools' computer networks. Given the limited amount of time the technology specialist will have in each school, which of the following measures is most appropriate for the specialist to take with regard to network problems?

    A. Requesting that a trained staff person be present at all times in each of the schools' computer labs so that problems are less likely to occur

    B. Giving all of the teachers administrator-level access to the network so that any teacher can deal with problems when they arise

    C. Training an individual or group of individuals on the first steps to take to resolve a problem before calling the specialist

    D. Ensuring that staff members know how to reach the specialist at all times so that he or she can deal with the problem as soon as possible

15.____

Use the information below to answer Questions 16 and 17:

A public school is developing an Educational Technology Improvement Team, which will be led by the school's principal and the educational technology specialist. The team will include teachers, staff and parents, as well as members of the local business community, all of whom will work together in partnership to guide the school through the improvement process. Members of the team will attend regular meetings to help design and implement a five-year strategic plan to improve the school's access to and use of educational technology.

16. For the partnerships established within the Educational Technology Improvement Team to be successful, it is most important that

    A. the roles, responsibilities and expectations of each team member are clearly defined

    B. each team member agrees to participate in a minimum number of meetings

    C. team members receive public recognition for their contributions

    D. each team member be allowed to speak publicly for the group

16.____

17. When considering potential Educational Technology Improvement Team members from the business community, it is most important for the school to ask which of the following questions?

    A. Will teachers, staff and parents be responsive to the advice and direction given by the potential team member?

    B. Is the potential team member likely to make significant financial contributions in addition to giving his or her time and expertise?

    C. Will the school's partnership with the potential team member be supported by the larger business community?

    D. Is the potential team member willing to make a long-term commitment to the improvement process?

17.____

KEY (CORRECT ANSWERS)

1.	D	11.	D
2.	A	12.	B
3.	A	13.	D
4.	C	14.	D
5.	B	15.	C
6.	A	16.	A
7.	A	17.	D
8.	B		
9.	C		
10.	B		

———

EXAMINATION SECTION

TEST 1

DIRECTIONS: Each question or incomplete statement is followed by several suggested
answers or completions. Select the one that BEST answers the question or
completes the statement. *PRINT THE LETTER OF THE CORRECT ANSWER
IN THE SPACE AT THE RIGHT.*

1.   A disk error is caused by   1.____
     A. slow processor   B. faulty RAM
     C. settings issue of CMOS   D. all of the above

2.   10/100 in network interface means   2.____
     A. protocol speed   B. mega bit per second
     C. fiber speed   D. server speed

3.   The tracks of hardware is subdivided as   3.____
     A. vectors   B. disks   C. sectors   D. clusters

4.   ESD damages the   4.____
     A. power supply   B. expansion board
     C. keyboard   D. monitor

5.   On the I/O card, the _____ drive has the 34 pin.   5.____
     A. floppy   B. SCSI   C. IDE   D. all of the above

6.   In case of a failure of power supply, what kind of beep will you hear?   6.____
     A. Short beep   B. One long beep
     C. Continuous long beeps   D. All of the above

7.   Which of the following adapters will you set before you install a SCSI CD-ROM?   7.____
     A. An unused SCSI address   B. B0007
     C. SCSI ID-1   D. None of the above

8.   What would you use to evaluate the serial and parallel ports?   8.____
     A. High volt probe   B. Cable scanner
     C. Loop backs   D. Sniffer

9.   An error message of 17xx means a problem with   9.____
     A. CMOS   B. ROM BIOS
     C. DMA control   D. hard drive

10. The bi-directional bus is called a _____ bus.   10.____
     A. data   B. control   C. address   D. multiplexed

11. _____ defines the quality of the printer output.
    A. Dot per inch   B. Dot per square inch
    C. Dots printed per unit time   D. Dots pixel
                                                 11._____

12. What would you do if APM stops functioning?
    A. Uncheck "enable advanced printing feature"
    B. Check "print spooled documents first"
    C. Check "start printing after last page"
    D. All of the above
                                                 12._____

13. What would you do to import XML incorporating GUID to a tally?
    A. Transfer data into MS Excel sheet and import to tally account
    B. Import Export Menu
    C. Both A and B
    D. None of the above
                                                 13._____

14. The writing device of Palm is called a
    A. stylus   B. pointer
    C. cursor   D. none of the above
                                                 14._____

15. A USB port of a computer has the ability to connect _____ number of devices.
    A. 12   B. 154   C. 127   D. 8
                                                 15._____

16. A _____ problem causes a system to not boot and beep.
    A. motherboard   B. RAM   C. BIOS   D. hard disk
                                                 16._____

17. What would you do if the computer cannot access the website in the corporate setting?
    A. Take a look at the proxy server   B. Check user authentication
    C. Ping Hosts   D. Check firewall
                                                 17._____

18. Which of the following is used to measure the database size?
    A. The total disk space
    B. Select sum (bytes)/1024/1024 from dba_data_files
    C. Both A and B
    D. None of the above
                                                 18._____

19. RAID defines
    A. fault tolerance   B. data transfer rate
    C. random access memory   D. read AID
                                                 19._____

20. The hard disk is measured in
    A. GHz   B. GB   C. Gwatts   D. MB
                                                 20._____

21. _____ cannot be shared over a network.
    A. Floppy   B. Keyword   C. Printer   D. CPU
                                                 21._____

22. Access does not support
    A. number   B. picture   C. memo   D. text

22.____

23. A network map shows
    A. devices and computers on network
    B. the location of your computer on the network
    C. information about the network
    D. none of the above

23.____

24. While making a chart in MS Word, the categories are shown on
    A. X axis   B. Y axis
    C. none of the above   D. both A and B

24.____

25. What would you do if Google Chrome does not open on a corporate computer?
    A. Turn off the antivirus temporarily   B. Check date settings of computer
    C. Check settings of antivirus   D. All of the above

25.____

KEY (CORRECT ANSWERS)

1.	D		11.	B
2.	B		12.	D
3.	C		13.	C
4.	B		14.	A
5.	A		15.	C
6.	D		16.	B
7.	A		17.	A
8.	C		18.	C
9.	D		19.	A
10.	A		20.	B

21.	D
22.	B
23.	A
24.	D
25.	D

TEST 2

DIRECTIONS: Each question or incomplete statement is followed by several suggested answers or completions. Select the one that BEST answers the question or completes the statement. *PRINT THE LETTER OF THE CORRECT ANSWER IN THE SPACE AT THE RIGHT.*

1. _____ is the computer's default IP address.
   A. 192.168.1.1   B. 255.000.1
   C. 01010101   D. None of the above
          1.____

2. Which of the following is a scheduling algorithm?
   A. FCFS   B. SJF
   C. RR   D. All of the above
          2.____

3. The trouble with the Shortest Job First algorithm is
   A. too long to be an effective algorithm
   B. to evaluate the next CPU request
   C. too complex
   D. all of the above
          3.____

4. ADSL contains _____ as the largest bandwidth.
   A. voice communication   B. upstream data
   C. downstream data   D. control data
          4.____

5. A Toshiba satellite ST1313 running Windows XP has trouble playing sounds. What would you do?
   A. Download sound driver for Realtek
   B. Install default Windows Vista
   C. Change sound card
   D. Change the speaker
          5.____

6. What would you do if your Wi-Fi keeps disconnecting?
   A. Check to see if computer is in the range of Wi-Fi
   B. Install the latest PC wireless card
   C. Click troubleshoot problems
   D. All of the above
          6.____

7. If your attachment in an e-mail is not opening, what is the problem?
   A. You don't have the software to open the file
   B. Your computer clock is at fault
   C. Your software is not compatible with the OS
   D. All of the above
          7.____

8. A DIMM has _____ number of pins.
   A. 72   B. 32   C. 32 to 72   D. 71
          8.____

9. What is the frequency of the SDRAM clock?   9.____
   A. 122 Mhz   B. 133 Mhz   C. 82 Mhz   D. 122 Ghz

10. IRQ6 is connected to   10.____
    A. sound card   B. Com1   C. floppy   D. LPT1

11. You can check the availability of the IRQ while installing PCI NICS   11.____
    through
    A. dip switches   B. CONFIG.SYS
    C. jumper setting   D. BIOS

12. What would you use if you have a smudged keyboard?   12.____
    A. TMC solvent   B. Silicone spray
    C. Alcohol   D. All-purpose cleaner

13. Which port would you switch to if the laser printer is working slow?   13.____
    A. RS232   B. SCSI   C. Serial   D. Parallel

14. If a mouse is moving erratically, the problem is   14.____
    A. dirty ball   B. faulty connection
    C. faulty driver   D. faulty IRQ setting

15. If a dot matrix printer quality is light, it is an issue of   15.____
    A. paper quality   B. faulty ribbon advancement
    C. head position   D. low cartridge

16. When configuring the hard drive, what would you do after low-level format?   16.____
    A. Formatting the DOS partition   B. Install OS
    C. Hard disk partition   D. None of the above

17. Which of the following errors means a change in two or more bits of data?   17.____
    A. Burst   B. Double bit
    C. Single bit   D. All of the above

18. Pentium system voltage is _____ volts.   18.____
    A. +12   B. +5   C. +8   D. +3.3

19. What would you do if the IDE hard drive is not recognized by the system   19.____
    after installation?
    A. Install drivers   B. Check the jumpers on hard disk
    C. Check information of hard disk   D. All of the above

20. What would you do to abort a deadlock?   20.____
    A. Terminate deadlock process
    B. Terminate the programs one by one
    C. Terminate programs at once
    D. All of the above

21. What would you do if you cannot share files over the network?   21.____
    A. Check network discovery   B. Check Share files
    C. Check password protection   D. All of the above

22. How would you protect a corporate computer from losing data due to a utility power   22.____
    blackout?
    A. Install a surge protector
    B. Install uninterrupted power supply
    C. Reduce power consumption
    D. All of the above

23. What would you do if the network key is lost?   23.____
    A. Install the latest network   B. Clear cache
    C. Set up the router again   D. None of the above

24. What settings prevent issues if you forget the password to log into Windows?   24.____
    A. Check use account and family safety
    B. Boot in to install disk and rest password
    C. Both A and B
    D. None of the above

25. What would you do to troubleshoot a computer monitor?   25.____
    A. Turn off the power supply   B. Hold down the power button
    C. Check settings of the monitor   D. All of the above

KEY (CORRECT ANSWERS)

1.	A		11.	D
2.	D		12.	D
3.	B		13.	D
4.	A		14.	A
5.	A		15.	B
6.	D		16.	A
7.	A		17.	A
8.	A		18.	D
9.	B		19.	B
10.	C		20.	C

21.	D
22.	D
23.	C
24.	A
25.	B

TEST 3

DIRECTIONS: Each question or incomplete statement is followed by several suggested answers or completions. Select the one that BEST answers the question or completes the statement. *PRINT THE LETTER OF THE CORRECT ANSWER IN THE SPACE AT THE RIGHT.*

1. What would you do if your monitor has no display while it is getting power?   1.____
   A. Check picture settings   B. Switch to a functional monitor
   C. Check video card   D. All of the above

2. How would you troubleshoot DirectX?   2.____
   A. Install DirectX diagnostic tool   B. Run troubleshoot
   C. Re-install DirectX   D. All of the above

3. What would you do if there is a conflict of network IP address?   3.____
   A. Convert Static IP address to DHCP
   B. Exclude Static IP address from DHCP server
   C. Both A and B
   D. None of the above

4. _____ defines the time interval between process submission and completion.   4.____
   A. Waiting time   B. Turnaround time
   C. Response time   D. Throughput

5. Mutual exclusion _____ for a non-sharable device including printers.   5.____
   A. must exist   B. must not exist
   C. may exist   D. may not exist

6. A kernel cannot schedule   6.____
   A. kernel level thread   B. user level thread
   C. process   D. all of the above

7. What would you do if the computer is not able to find the C: drive when you   7.____
   boot?
   A. Swap hard drives to identify the issue
   B. Reboot
   C. Put your hard drive in a bag and place it in a freezer for the night
   D. All of the above

8. Data security does not need a   8.____
   A. big RAM   B. strong password
   C. audit log   D. scan

9. What would you do if you get an error message that prompts, "Cannot obtain IP"?
    A. Open command prompt
    B. Type "ipconfig/renew" in the command prompt
    C. Click the troubleshoot network
    D. All of the above

9.____

10. _____ should be used to transfer large data.
    A. DMA   B. Programmed I/O
    C. Controller register   D. LPT1

10.____

11. What would you do after recovery from a system failure?
    A. Repair ingeneration of the system
    B. Notify the parties at both ends
    C. Adjust the recovery system
    D. Systematically log failures

11.____

12. _____ is not present in a computer.
    A. USB port   B. Parallel port
    C. ROM   D. Com1/Com2

12.____

13. _____ produces a print with pins of grid.
    A. Inkjet   B. Laser
    C. Daisy wheel   D. Dot matrix

13.____

14. What would you do if Windows Vista/7/XP does not sleep?
    A. Check settings of the device manager
    B. Uncheck all the options that wakes up the computer
    C. Look for advanced power management
    D. All of the above

14.____

15. What is the use of the System File Checker tool?
    A. Replace missing files   B. Replace corrupt files
    C. Scan drive   D. All of the above

15.____

16. What would you do if the PC reboots between the processes of updating?
    A. Undo updates by System Restore
    B. Go to recovery options
    C. Press F8 and select "repair your computer"
    D. All of the above

16.____

17. What would you do if there is no sound in a PC?
    A. Verify the settings   B. Select default in Playback
    C. Check speaker cables   D. All of the above

17.____

18. _____ keeps a record of the major events such as warning and errors.
    A. Event viewer   B. Windows
    C. Windows Vista   D. ALU

18.____

3 (#3)

19. A run time error "DLL is not supported" means 19.____
    A. bad installation   B. corrupt MS Word
    C. low memory   D. all of the above

20. What would you do if the system gives error MSGSRV32 after 20.____
recovering from power?
    A. Disable all programs using SETI   B. Disable power management
    C. Reboot computer   D. All of the above

21. While encrypting Windows XP files, you see "Encrypt contents to secure 21.____
data" as grey. What is the possible reason?
    A. Using Windows XP home edition
    B. The hard drive is not NTFS formatted
    C. The hard drive is FAT32 file system
    D. All of the above

22. You get _____ error message if you are installing a program from a CD 22.____
that is not clean.
    A. Win 32 application   B. Is not a valid Win 32 application
    C. Missing File Win 32   D. None of the above

23. What does it mean when the printer is blinking? 23.____
    A. Printer error   B. Printer ready
    C. Printer is processing   D. Printer is working

24. If MCI CD audio driver is not installed, the computer will 24.____
    A. not play audio CDs   B. mute DVD
    C. both A and B   D. none of the above

25. What would you do if the computer plug is emitting sparks? 25.____
    A. Disconnect all peripheral devices from the computer
    B. Change the power cord
    C. Check the power supply
    D. All of the above

KEY (CORRECT ANSWERS)

1.	D		11.	A
2.	A		12.	D
3.	C		13.	D
4.	B		14.	D
5.	A		15.	D
6.	B		16.	D
7.	D		17.	D
8.	A		18.	A
9.	B		19.	A
10.	A		20.	A

21.	D
22.	B
23.	A
24.	A
25.	D

TEST 4

DIRECTIONS: Each question or incomplete statement is followed by several suggested answers or completions. Select the one that BEST answers the question or completes the statement. *PRINT THE LETTER OF THE CORRECT ANSWER IN THE SPACE AT THE RIGHT.*

1. How would you find out the APM version of Windows?   1.____
   A. Device Manager tab in the systems
   B. Install Advanced Power Management
   C. Check settings of control panel
   D. All of the above

2. How would you find the AMI POST beep codes?   2.____
   A. On the beep code page   B. On the CPU
   C. Settings   D. All of the above

3. MemTest86 is a _____ diagnostic tool.   3.____
   A. USB   B. bootable
   C. ineffective   D. all of the above

4. If you experience slow performance of your computer, the problem is   4.____
   A. RAM   B. processor   C. ROM   D. Throughput

5. How do you remove a RAM module?   5.____
   A. Pressing the small levers at both ends of the module
   B. Click safely remove hardware
   C. You cannot remove a RAM
   D. By uninstalling the RAM

6. How do you connect the computer clock with the Internet?   6.____
   A. By installing an Internet clock
   B. By setting the date in Time option in the control panel
   C. Processing the clock
   D. All of the above

7. To remove and re-install the real-time clock, you have to run the system on   7.____
   A. power   B. safe mode
   C. normal mode   D. all of the above

8. To keep track of the time, a computer has a battery called   8.____
   A. CMOS   B. CMAS   C. CMSC   D. CDMA

9. What is the problem if the graphic card is heating?   9.____
   A. Faulty motherboard   B. Driver issues
   C. Outdated BIOS   D. Faulty fan

10. What should you know or do before removing a failed PC power supply?   10.____
    A. ESD procedures   B. Disconnect all connectors
    C. Both A and B   D. None of the above

11. _____ drive has the faster data transfer rate.   11.____
    A. IDE   B. SSD   C. SATA   D. Flash

12. SATA and IDE are two different types of ports used to connect   12.____
    A. storage devices   B. RAM
    C. ROM   D. graphic memory

13. Which of the following mediums cannot be used to install OS?   13.____
    A. CD/DVD ROM   B. USB flash drive
    C. Floppy disk   D. RAM

14. Which Windows is touch optimized?   14.____
    A. Windows ME   B. Windows 8
    C. Windows Vista   D. Windows 98

15. What is the other name used for a USB flash drive?   15.____
    A. Pen Drive   B. Thumb Drive
    C. Flash Disk   D. All of the above

16. RATS is defined as   16.____
    A. Regression Analysis Time Series   B. Regression Analysis Time Sharing
    C. Real Analysis Series   D. Real Analysis Time Series

17. _____ keeps a record of the major events such as warning and errors.   17.____
    A. Event viewer   B. Windows
    C. Windows Vista   D. ALU

18. You must use a _____ to notify Windows that you are about to uninstall   18.____
    Plug and Play devices.
    A. Device Manager   B. Device Driver
    C. Control Panel   D. Both A and B

19. _____ is used for data entry storage but not for processing.   19.____
    A. Mouse   B. Dumb Terminal
    C. Micro computer   D. Dedicated data entry system

20. Which of the following is NOT a PnP device?   20.____
    A. Mouse   B. Printer   C. Keyboard   D. Joystick

21. WindowsKey + R takes you to   21.____
    A. Run   B. Device Manager
    C. Hardware components   D. None of the above

22. Which of the following has no dipswitches? 22.____
    A. Zorro Device   B. Micro channel
    C. NuBus   D. All of the above

23. Use _____ to ensure security holes are patched. 23.____
    A. automatic updates   B. password
    C. both A and B   D. none of the above

24. What would you do if the speaker is not working? 24.____
    A. Check connectors   B. Check power supply
    C. Check sound card   D. All of the above

25. You get a message abclink.xyz when starting your computer. What would you do? 25.____
    A. Press any key to continue   B. Check settings
    C. Uninstall a program   D. All of the above

KEY (CORRECT ANSWERS)

1.	A		11.	B
2.	A		12.	A
3.	B		13.	D
4.	A		14.	B
5.	A		15.	D
6.	B		16.	A
7.	C		17.	A
8.	A		18.	A
9.	D		19.	B
10.	C		20.	B

21. A
22. A
23. A
24. D
25. D

EXAMINATION SECTION

TEST 1

DIRECTIONS: Each question or incomplete statement is followed by several suggested answers or completions. Select the one that BEST answers the question or completes the statement. *PRINT THE LETTER OF THE CORRECT ANSWER IN THE SPACE AT THE RIGHT.*

1. What is the default compressing software of Windows?   1.____
    A. WinRar   B. 7-zip
    C. WinZip   D. All of the above

2. Which software does NOT require special drives to run?   2.____
    A. Mouse   B. Keyboard
    C. Joystick   D. All of the above

3. What software is required to run PDF?   3.____
    A. MS Word   B. Windows Media Player
    C. Adobe Photoshop   D. Adobe Reader

4. An error message that says "there is a problem with this website's security certificate"   4.____
    appears when
    A. Windows is outdated   B. browser is outdated
    C. date and time are wrong   D. internet is disabled

5. Software should always be _____ for better performance.   5.____
    A. disabled   B. updated
    C. uninstalled   D. all of the above

6. SATA is the abbreviation for   6.____
    A. Sequential Advanced Technology Advancement
    B. Serial Advanced Technology Attachment
    C. Serial Automatic Technology Attachment
    D. Supper Advanced Technology Attachment

7. Which of the following is a part of management software development?   7.____
    A. People   B. Product
    C. Process   D. All of the above

8. _____ is a tool in the design phase.   8.____
    A. Abstraction   B. Refinement
    C. Information Hiding   D. All of the above

9. What is the other name used for white box software testing technique?   9.____
    A. Basic Path   B. Graph Testing
    C. Data Flow   D. Glass Box Testing

10. _____ is included in the Turnkey package.   10.____
    A. Software   B. Hardware
    C. Training   D. All of the above

11. _____ are types of a record access method.   11.____
    A. Sequential and random   B. Direct and immediate
    C. Sequential and indexed   D. Online and real time

12. _____ has a sequential file organization.   12.____
    A. Grocery store checkout   B. Bank checking account
    C. Payroll   D. Airline reservation

13. What will you recommend when users are involved in complex tasks?   13.____
    A. A short term memory   B. Demands on shortcut usage
    C. Both A and B   D. None of the above

14. _____ protocols are similar to HTTP.   14.____
    A. FTP; SMTP   B. FTP; SNMP
    C. FTP; MTV   D. SMTP; SNMP

15. _____ is the oldest data model.   15.____
    A. Relational   B. Deductive
    C. Physical   D. Hierarchical

16. _____ defines the transaction executed.   16.____
    A. Committed   B. Aborted
    C. Failed   D. Rolled Back

17. _____ is NOT a deadlock managing strategy.   17.____
    A. Deadlock prevention   B. Timeout
    C. Deadlock detection   D. Deadlock annihilation

18. _____ is the average execution time of the monitor power process.   18.____
    A. 1 ms   B. 10 ms
    C. 100 ms   D. None of the above

19. _____ is NOT a dimension of scalability.   19.____
    A. Size   B. Distribution
    C. Interception   D. Manageability

20. What would you do if the icons on the desktop are white or missing colors?   20.____
    A. End the explorer.exe   B. Check settings in Appearance
    C. Both A and B   D. None of the above

21. What would you do if while using AutoCAD you receive a message of "license is invalid"?   21.____
    A. Delete licensing file   B. Re-enter registration information
    C. Both A and B   D. None of the above

22. What would you do to satisfy the growing communication need in your   22._____
    company?
    A. Use front end processor   B. Use a multiplexer
    C. Use a controller   D. All of the above

23. _____ is a part of x.25.   23._____
    A. Technique for start stop data B. Technique for dial access
    C. DTE/DCE interface   D. None of the above

24. Which of the following is a software product?   24._____
    A. CAD, Cam   B. Firmware, Embedded
    C. Generic, Customized   D. Both A and B

25. ACT in Boehm software maintenance model is the abbreviation for   25._____
    A. Actual Change Track   B. Annual Change Track
    C. Annual Change Traffic   D. Actual Change Traffic

KEY (CORRECT ANSWERS)

1.	C		11.	A
2.	D		12.	B
3.	D		13.	A
4.	C		14.	A
5.	B		15.	D
6.	B		16.	A
7.	D		17.	D
8.	D		18.	A
9.	D		19.	D
10.	D		20.	C

21.	C
22.	D
23.	C
24.	C
25.	C

TEST 2

DIRECTIONS: Each question or incomplete statement is followed by several suggested answers or completions. Select the one that BEST answers the question or completes the statement. *PRINT THE LETTER OF THE CORRECT ANSWER IN THE SPACE AT THE RIGHT.*

1. Software maintenance incorporates
   A. Error Correction
   B. Enhancement of capabilities
   C. Deletion of obsolete capabilities
   D. All of the above

   1._____

2. Software Maintenance model called Taute has _____ number of phases.
   A. 6   B. 7   C. 8   D. 9

   2._____

3. _____ is a software process certification.
   A. JAVA certified
   B. IBM certified
   C. ISO-9000
   D. Microsoft certified

   3._____

4. _____ is known as quality management in software development.
   A. SQA
   B. SQM
   C. SQI
   D. Both A and B

   4._____

5. Software reliability means
   A. time   B. efficiency   C. quality   D. speed

   5._____

6. A software package designed to store and manage databases is
   A. Database   B. DBMS   C. Data Model   D. Data

   6._____

7.

   The above image represents a _____ relation.
   A. many to many
   B. many to one
   C. one to one
   D. one to many

   7._____

8. The diagram shown at the right indicates that
   A. there is a missing entity
   B. students attend courses
   C. many students can attend many courses
   D. students have to attend more than one course

   8._____

9. In relational algebra, the union of two sets (set A and set B) corresponds to
   A. A OR B   B. A + B   C. A AND B   D. A - B

   9._____

10. _____ is the location of the keyboard status byte.   10._____
    A. 0040:0000H   B. 0040:0013H
    C. 0040:0015H   D. 0040:0017H

11. What is the number of maximum interrupts occurring in a PC?   11._____
    A. 64   B. 128   C. 256   D. 512

12. How many bytes are there in an operating system name in the boot block?   12._____
    A. 3   B. 5   C. 8   D. 11

13. What is the size of a DPB structure?   13._____
    A. 16   B. 32   C. 64   D. 128

14. _____ is the file system in CD.   14._____
    A. Contiguous   B. Chained   C. Indexed   D. None

15. NTFS volume is accessed directly in   15._____
    A. DOS   B. Linux   C. Windows   D. MAC

16. _____.com is an MS DOS file in the boot disk.   16._____
    A. Command   B. Start   C. Tree   D. Ver

17. _____ is a table in the OS that keeps information of files.   17._____
    A. FFT   B. FIT   C. FAT   D. DIT

18. _____ is a system programming language.   18._____
    A. C   B. PL/360
    C. PASCAL   D. All of the above

19. What would you do if the icons disappear from the Taskbar?   19._____
    A. Press Windows Key + R and type "regedit"
    B. Delete Icon stream and past icon Stream values
    C. Uncheck user interface
    D. All of the above

20. What would you do if you want to make sure the drivers of the old printers   20._____
    are removed?
    A. Check Server Properties   B. Check settings in Appearance
    C. Both A and B   D. None of the above

21. Microsoft has introduced _____ tool that incorporates all the automated fixes.   21._____
    A. Fix It Center   B. Fix All
    C. Fixing It   D. none of the above

22. A PC can only use one _____ device at a time.   22._____
    A. Ready Boost   B. Built-in Flash
    C. RAM   D. all of the above

23. You need to edit two registry keys called _____ if you cannot customize   23.____
     folders.
     A. bagMRU and Bags   B. RAM and ROM
     C. DTE/DCE interface   D. none of the above

24. What would you do if your PC does not have a Windows Installation disk?   24.____
     A. Select "create a system repair" disc
     B. Place a DVD in the writeable drive
     C. Create a bootable disc by the "Repair Your Computer"
     D. All of the above

25. Code of conduct defines the   25.____
     A. employees' legal and ethical obligations
     B. commitment to integrity
     C. terms and condition of the company
     D. legal contract

_____

KEY (CORRECT ANSWERS)

1.	D		11.	C
2.	C		12.	C
3.	C		13.	B
4.	A		14.	A
5.	A		15.	A
6.	B		16.	A
7.	D		17.	A
8.	C		18.	D
9.	B		19.	D
10.	D		20.	C

21.	A
22.	A
23.	A
24.	D
25.	A

_____

TEST 3

DIRECTIONS: Each question or incomplete statement is followed by several suggested answers or completions. Select the one that BEST answers the question or completes the statement. *PRINT THE LETTER OF THE CORRECT ANSWER IN THE SPACE AT THE RIGHT.*

1. What would you do if the drive does not open by double-clicking?   1.____
   A. Check search option in drive C
   B. Enter regsvr32/I shell32.dll in the Run
   C. Check settings in the control panel
   D. Both A and B

2. What would you do if you attach another display unit to your PC but it remains   2.____
   blank?
   A. Check the cables
   B. Check display properties
   C. Select the properties to duplicate each other
   D. All of the above

3. _____ helps you when you are locked out of Manager and Registry Editor?   3.____
   A. Virus Effect Remover   B. Fix It Tool
   C. Safe mode   D. All of the above

4. The two types of cache memory in RAM are called   4.____
   A. ALU and CPU   B. Buffer and Procedure
   C. Date and Timing   D. DLL and STAT

5. _____ points at the same location when the keyboard buffer is empty.   5.____
   A. Interrupt   B. Head and Tail
   C. Tail   D. All of the above

6. _____ frequency is divided by the interval time.   6.____
   A. Output   B. Input
   C. Both A and B   D. None of the above
   E. All of the above

7. What is the number of PPI present in a standard PC?   7.____
   A. 1   B. 4   C. 8   D. 16

8. _____ is used as a status port of the keyboard.   8.____
   A. 64H   B. 44H
   C. 77H   D. All of the above

9. _____ is a computer with an 80286 microprocessor.   9.____
   A. XT computer   B. PC/AT computer
   C. PS/2 computer   D. None of the above

10. _____ is not a process.
   A. Arranging
   B. Manipulation
   C. Calculating
   D. Gathering

   10.____

11. _____ is a sequential processing application.
   A. Grades processing
   B. Payroll processing
   C. Both A and B
   D. All of the above

   11.____

12. _____ has a record disk address.
   A. Track Number
   B. Sector Number
   C. Surface Number
   D. All of the above

   12.____

13. Which printer would you NOT use while printing on a carbon form?
   A. Daisy Wheel
   B. Dot Matrix
   C. Laser
   D. None of the above

   13.____

14. A(n) _____ produces the BEST quality graphic production.
   A. laser printer
   B. inkjet printer
   C. plotter
   D. dot matrix

   14.____

15. _____ allows both read and write operations at the same time.
   A. ROM
   B. RAM
   C. EPROM
   D. None of the above

   15.____

16. _____ has the shortest access time.
   A. Cache Memory
   B. Magnetic Bubble Memory
   C. Magnetic Core Memory
   D. RAM

   16.____

17. _____ defines the status of resources assigned to the process.
   A. Process Control
   B. ALU
   C. Register Unit
   D. Process Description

   17.____

18. Memory _____ controls access to the memory.
   A. map
   B. protection
   C. management
   D. instruction

   18.____

19. _____ is able to record and track all the information in a database about animal movement once placed on the animal.
   A. POS   B. RFID   C. PPS   D. GPS

   19.____

20. The print of a picture taken from a digital camera is said to be a(n)
   A. data
   B. output
   C. input
   D. none of the above

   20.____

21. _____ are the two types of record access methods.
   A. Sequential and Random
   B. Direct and Immediate
   C. Online and Real Time
   D. None of the above

   21.____

22. _____ is the most efficient method of file organization when the file is highly active.

    A. ISAM   B. VSAM
    C. B-Tree   D. All of the above

22._____

23. _____ is the standard approach for storing data.

    A. MIS   B. Structured Programming
    C. CODASYL specification   D. None of the above

23._____

24. Which of the following RDBMS supports client server application development?

    A. dBase V   B. Oracle 7.1
    C. FoxPro 2.1   D. Both A and B

24._____

25. Which of the following techniques would you use to find the location of the element?

    A. Traversal   B. Search
    C. Sort   D. None of the above

25._____

KEY (CORRECT ANSWERS)

1.	D		11.	C
2.	D		12.	D
3.	A		13.	C
4.	B		14.	C
5.	B		15.	B
6.	B		16.	A
7.	B		17.	D
8.	A		18.	A
9.	B		19.	B
10.	D		20.	B

21.	A
22.	A
23.	C
24.	B
25.	B

TEST 4

DIRECTIONS: Each question or incomplete statement is followed by several suggested answers or completions. Select the one that BEST answers the question or completes the statement. *PRINT THE LETTER OF THE CORRECT ANSWER IN THE SPACE AT THE RIGHT.*

1. A band is equal to
    A. a byte   B. a bit
    C. 100 bits   D. none of the above

    1.____

2. The number of zeroes in each symbol in an odd-parity is
    A. odd   B. even
    D. unknown   D. both A and B

    2.____

3. _____ is also called an IPng.
    A. IPv4   B. IPv5
    C. IPv6   D. All of the above

    3.____

4. IPv6 addresses are written in
    A. hexadecimal   B. binary
    C. decimal   D. none of the above

    4.____

5. Green PCs are designed to
    A. minimize power consumption   B. minimize inactive components
    C. minimize electricity bill   D. all of the above

    5.____

6. Hyper V Network Virtualizations do not have the ability to access the outside world unless you
    A. implement a forwarding agent   B. implement a gateway
    C. implement a CISCO NEXUS   D. None of the above
    E. All of the above

    6.____

7. What would you do to create a shortcut of a website on the desktop?
    A. Left click on the icon present on the left side of the address bar and drag it to the desktop
    B. Save the webpage through the Save Page As
    C. Bookmark the page
    D. All of the above

    7.____

8. E-mail, word documents, web pages, video and photos are called unstructured data because
    A. they consist of text and multimedia
    B. the data cannot be stored in a database
    C. they cannot be stored in row and columns
    D. all of the above

    8.____

9. What would you do to manage corporate unstructured data?   9.____
    A. Install big data tool software
    B. Install data integration tools
    C. Install business intelligence software
    D. All of the above

10. Software-defined data center is a concept for   10.____
    A. a virtualized infrastructure
    B. fully automated control of data
    C. hardware maintenance through intelligent software
    D. all of the above

11. What is a cloud database?   11.____
    A. Internet based database provided through cloud data server
    B. Database-as-a-Service
    C. Both A and B
    D. None of the above

12. Monitor footprint refers to the   12.____
    A. disk space of your PC
    B. map of the monitor
    C. space taken up by the monitor on the desk
    D. footprints of the monitor

13. NOS are already built in   13.____
    A. UNIX   B. Mac OS
    C. Windows NT   D. Both A and B

14. _____ is an example of a network monitoring tool.   14.____
    A. Ping   B. VoIP
    C. POP3 server   D. All of the above

15. Tomato is the name of a wireless router   15.____
    A. firmware   B. WRT54GS
    C. both A and B   D. none of the above

16. _____ is a combination of software and hardware.   16.____
    A. Firmware   B. PROM
    C. EPROMs   D. All of the above

17. Object-oriented fonts are also called   17.____
    A. scalable fonts   B. vector fonts
    C. both A and B   D. screen fonts

18. What is the issue if the computer is rebooting itself?   18.____
    A. Faulty power supply   B. Faulty cooling fan
    C. Dirt on the cooling fan   D. All of the above

19. What is the meaning if you receive a message "system running low on virtual memory"?

    A. The system is low on RAM   B. The hard disc is full

    C. Both A and B   D. None of the above

19.____

20. Your computer freezes on startup. What is the issue?

    A. Defective hardware   B. Faulty software

    C. Bugged OS   D. All of the above

20.____

21. The computer software maintenance checklist consists of

    A. update virus or install antivirus   B. delete temporary internet file

    C. clear internet cache   D. all of the above

21.____

22. A CRC error is caused by

    A. a scratched DVD on disk   B. dirt on CD/DVD

    C. partially burned CDs   D. all of the above

22.____

23. An error message "an invalid Windows File" means

    A. incomplete download   B. system crash

    C. software bug   D. all of the above

23.____

24. What would you do if it is taking longer than usual to copy files in Windows?

    A. Install an external file such as TeraCopy

    B. Resume broken files

    C. Increase RAM

    D. Both A and B

24.____

25. _____ software will help you protect file and folders.

    A. HideFolder   B. Truecrypt

    C. TeraCopy   D. None of the above

25.____

KEY (CORRECT ANSWERS)

1.	D		11.	C
2.	C		12.	C
3.	C		13.	D
4.	A		14.	D
5.	A		15.	A
6.	A		16.	A
7.	A		17.	C
8.	D		18.	D
9.	D		19.	A
10.	D		20.	D

21.	D
22.	D
23.	D
24.	A
25.	B

EXAMINATION SECTION
TEST 1

DIRECTIONS: Each question or incomplete statement is followed by several suggested answers or completions. Select the one that BEST answers the question or completes the statement. *PRINT THE LETTER OF THE CORRECT ANSWER IN THE SPACE AT THE RIGHT.*

1. _____ is the data that has been organized or presented in a meaningful fashion.   1.____
    A. A process   B. Software   C. Storage   D. Information

2. Of the following data processing functions, which one is NOT a data   2.____
    processing function of a computer?
    A. Data gathering   B. Processing data into information
    C. Analyzing the data or information   D. Storing the data or information

3. In electronic data processing systems, which standard data code is used   3.____
    commonly to represent alphabetical, numerical and punctuation characters?
    A. ASCII   B. EBCDIC   C. BCD   D. All of the above

4. Data processing performed by several separate computers/networks, at   4.____
    several different locations, linked by a communications facility is known as
    _____ processing.
    A. distributed   B. centralized   C. on-line   D. batch

5. Which process is utilized by large retailers to study market trends?   5.____
    A. Data conversion   B. Data mining
    C. Data selection   D. Pos

6. In normalization, second normal form (2NF) eliminates in Tables   6.____
    A. all hidden dependencies
    B. the possibility of insertion anomalies
    C. all non-key fields depend on the whole primary key
    D. none of the above

7. Which of the following is a bottom-up approach for database design which is   7.____
    designed by examining the relationship between attributes?
    A. Functional dependency   B. Normalization
    C. Decomposition   D. None of the above

8. Which is the process that is used to restore data that has been stored in a   8.____
    computer?
    A. Retrieve   B. Backup   C. Recovery   D. Deadlock

9. Which term BEST explains the homogenous data type?   9.____
   A. Data items of same length
   B. Data items of same type
   C. Data items of different length
   D. Numerical and character date items

10. For any category of data being processed and any type of device used for this   10.____
    purpose, all data processing systems perform the same steps. Which is the
    CORRECT sequence?
    A. Analyzing, coding and execution
    B. Input, processing and output
    C. Input, organizing and processing
    D. Processing, storage and distribution

11. Which of the following e-data processing methods works on data that   11.____
    is accumulated from more than location and records that are updated instantly?
    A. Minicomputer system   B. Batch processing system
    C. On-line, real-time system   D. Micro computer system

12. Suppose you are employed by the Air Transport Company to design a   12.____
    database for an airline transaction system. The database has to capture the
    detailed level of data related to the tickets booked by the user and the updating
    made by them with timestamp. Which database model would be your
    preference?
    A. Dimensional model
    B. It can be either dimensional model or on-line transaction processing
       model
    C. On-line transaction processing model
    D. None of the above

13. In the database management system, what are the after triggers functions?   13.____
    A. Triggers generated after a particular operation
    B. Triggers run after an insert, update or delete on a table
    C. Triggers run after an insert, views, update or delete on a table
    D. None of the above

14. For trigger creation, a CREATE TRIGGER statement is used. So, clause   14.____
    _____ specifies the table name on which the trigger is to be attached. Also,
    _____ specifies that it is an AFTER INSERT trigger.
    A. for insert; on   B. on; for insert
    C. for; insert   D. none of the above

15. Which part of a data flow diagram (DFD) represents the people and   15.____
    organizations that send data that the system being modeled uses or produces?
    A. Processes   B. Data source   C. Data store   D. Data flow

16. The purpose of cryptography is   16.____
    A. deadlock removal   B. job scheduling
    C. protection   D. file management

17. _____ memory allocation method suffers from external fragmentation.   17._____
    A. Segmentation   B. Demand paging
    C. Swapping   D. Paging

18. When working with a time-sharing operating system, when the time slot   18._____
    given to a process is completed, the process goes from the running state to the
    _____ state.
    A. blocked   B. ready   C. complete   D. terminated

19. The purpose of real-time systems   19._____
    A. is primarily used on mainframe computers
    B. monitors events instantly as they occur
    C. is employed in program development
    D. none of the above

20. What are the causes of process termination?   20._____
    A. Process is removed from all queues and process's PCB is de-allocated
    B. Process is completed
    C. Process control block is never de-allocated
    D. None of the above

21. Fragmentation of the file system   21._____
    A. occurs only if the file system is used improperly
    B. can always be prevented
    C. can be temporarily removed by compaction
    D. is a characteristic of all file systems

22. _____ scheduling is most suitable for a time-shared interactive system. It   22._____
    assigns the CPU to the first process in the ready queue for q time units. After q
    time units, if the process is not handed over to the CPU, it is blocked, and the
    process is put at the tail of the ready queue (done).
    A. Shortest-job-first (SJF)   B. CPU
    C. Round-robin (RR)   D. None of the above

23. Backup can BEST be explained as   23._____
    A. a tool that must be offered by Windows operating system like Windows
       XP and 7 that checks when your system hardware and software need a
       new OS
    B. copy files from a computer to another medium, such as tape, DVD,
       another hard drive, or a removable drive
    C. a term that is used to move from one operating system to another, which
       may or may not involve implementing a new computer
    D. none of the above

24. As a Technical Support Officer for a large organization, at times you have to deal with login authentication problems of user computers. Which of the following is NOT a best practice for password policy?
   A. Restriction on password reuse
   B. Password encryption
   C. Having changed passwords every two years
   D. Deciding maximum age of password
   E. None of the above
24.____

25. When working in a team environment, the BEST adopted problem-solving technique in which all members of a team fully accept and support a decision is
   A. compromise   B. goal
   C. consensus   D. none of the above
25.____

KEY (CORRECT ANSWERS)

1.	D		11.	C
2.	C		12.	C
3.	A		13.	B
4.	A		14.	B
5.	B		15.	B
6.	A		16.	C
7.	B		17.	A
8.	A		18.	B
9.	B		19.	B
10.	B		20.	A

21. A
22. C
23. B
24. C
25. C

TEST 2

DIRECTIONS: Each question or incomplete statement is followed by several suggested answers or completions. Select the one that BEST answers the question or completes the statement. *PRINT THE LETTER OF THE CORRECT ANSWER IN THE SPACE AT THE RIGHT.*

1. A collection of facts like drawings, pictures and stock figures is called   1._____
    A. quantity   B. product
    C. data   D. collector's item
    E. information

2. The electronic data processing technique that collects data into groups to permit   2._____
    convenient and efficient processing is known as
    A. document-count processing   B. batch-processing
    C. generalized-audit processing   D. multiprogramming

3. Lee runs a grocery store; he wants to keep a record of daily sold items. Lee   3._____
    uses a bar chart for this purpose to show many breads he sold per day. Each
    day has its own bar. How could he find the total number of breads sold?
    A. Finding the height of the tallest bar
    B. Adding together the heights of all the bars in the chart
    C. Counting the number of bars
    D. Finding the average of the values of each bar

4. A summary level view of a system and the highest-level DFD is provided to   4._____
    the reader with the help of
    A. data store   B. data source
    C. context diagram   D. documentation

5. Which option BEST explains the *triggers*?   5._____
    A. A statement that enables the start of any DBMS
    B. A statement that is executed by the user when debugging an application
        program
    C. A statement that is executed automatically by the system as a side effect
        of modification to the database
    D. None of the above

6. Virtual memory technique is implemented with the help of   6._____
    A. segmentation   B. fragmentation
    C. paging   D. none of the above

7. Which diagram is used to represent the relationship between the input,   7._____
    processing and output of an AIS?
    A. Flowchart   B. Data flow diagram
    C. Document flowchart   D. System flowcharts

8. _____ scheduling is the simplest scheduling technique that forces the short processes to wait for very long processes.
   - A. Round-robin (RR)
   - B. Last-in, first out (LIFO)
   - C. Shortest-job-first (SJF)
   - D. First-come, first-served (FCFS)

   8._____

9. Mapping of file is managed by
   - A. paging table
   - B. virtual memory
   - C. file system
   - D. file metadata

   9._____

10. On-line analytical processing is also called _____ processing.
    - A. decision support
    - B. on-line transactional
    - C. transaction control
    - D. none of the above

    10._____

11. When working in large organizations, you have to deal with different access authentication situations. To ensure security, you have multiple options in such conditions. Which of the following is the LEAST secure method of authentication for your organization?
    - A. Key card
    - B. Fingerprint
    - C. Retina pattern
    - D. Password

    11._____

12. DML stands for
    - A. data management language
    - B. data markup language
    - C. data manipulation language
    - D. none of the above

    12._____

13. Which term BEST explains the characteristics of a computer to run several operations simultaneously?
    - A. Concurrency   B. Deadlock   C. Backup   D. Recovery

    13._____

14. In DBMS, what is the BEST way to represent the attributes in a large database?
    - A. Relational-and
    - B. Concatenation
    - C. Dot representation
    - D. All of the above

    14._____

15. Database locking mechanism is used to rectify the problem of
    - A. lost update
    - B. uncommitted dependency
    - C. inconsistent data
    - D. none of the above

    15._____

16. In the scheme (dept name, size), we have relations (total inst 2010, total inst 2013). Which dependency has led to this relation?
    - A. Company name, year->size
    - B. Year->size
    - C. Company name->size
    - D. Size->year

    16._____

17. Which is the BEST possible option to evaluate any scheduling algorithm?
    - A. CPU utilization
    - B. Throughput
    - C. Waiting time
    - D. All of the above

    17._____

18. When the round robin CPU scheduling technique is adopted in a time-shared system,
    A. very large time slice degenerates into first-come, first-served algorithm
    B. extremely small time slices improve performance
    C. extremely small time slices degenerates into LIFO algorithm
    D. medium sized time slices leads to shortest request time first algorithm

18.____

19. A priority scheduling BIGGEST issue is
    A. definite blocking   B. starvation
    C. priority queues   D. none of the above

19.____

20.

The above figure is called a(n) _____ in use case diagram.
    A. person   B. substitute
    C. actor (symbol)   D. flow directive

20.____

21. Use case models can be summed up into
    A. use case diagram   B. use case description
    C. all of the above   D. none of the above

21.____

22. Prototype
    A. is a working model of different parts at different levels or all of a final product
    B. does not represent any sort of models
    C. can never consist of full size
    D. all of the above

22.____

23. Kim has been given some official documents to type. While typing, he notices that some of the words are automatically changing. He is very interested to understand the purpose of this feature in MS Word. AutoCorrect is designed to replace _____ words as you type.
    A. short, repetitive   B. grammatically incorrect
    C. misspelled   D. none of the above

23.____

24. As a computer associate, you have to write different reports like weekly departmental updates and specially designed tasks to analyze the different areas of an organization. Of the following, which is considered good reporting practices?
    A. Report factual observations, not opinions
    B. Identify proper personnel
    C. Formalize your inspection criteria
    D. None of the above

24.____

25. To improve the competency of teams, members of a(n) _____ team have   25.____
been cross-trained so that each person is capable of performing the duties of
all the other team members.
    A. functional   B. cross-functional
    C. multifunctional   D. self-directed

KEY (CORRECT ANSWERS)

1.	C		11.	D
2.	B		12.	C
3.	B		13.	A
4.	C		14.	B
5.	C		15.	C
6.	C		16.	A
7.	D		17.	D
8.	C		18.	A
9.	D		19.	B
10.	A		20.	C

21.	C
22.	A
23.	C
24.	A
25.	D

TEST 3

DIRECTIONS: Each question or incomplete statement is followed by several suggested answers or completions. Select the one that BEST answers the question or completes the statement. *PRINT THE LETTER OF THE CORRECT ANSWER IN THE SPACE AT THE RIGHT.*

1. Information is _____ unfinished data.   1.____
   A. always   B. not   C. occasionally   D. none of these

2. Which option BEST explains Beta software?   2.____
   A. An early development version of software in which there are likely to be bugs.
   B. Software will expire in 30 days after its download.
   C. Software that has successfully passed the alpha test stage.
   D. Up-gradation of software is not possible.

3. Jane drew a bar chart to show the number of different cars he saw daily on   3.____
   his way back home. There was no bar above the Mercedes. What does this mean?
   A. He did not see any Mercedes during his trip
   B. No Mercedes exist in his city
   C. He selected a wrong type of chart
   D. He has never seen a Mercedes before

4. A flowchart is a picture representation of a program. Flows should initiate   4.____
   from top to bottom and from right to left. This flowcharting principle is
   commonly known as the _____ rule.
   A. narrative   B. sandwich   C. direction   D. consistency

5. The database designing approach which is based on a bottom-up approach   5.____
   that is designed by examining the relationship between attributes is
   A. functional dependency   B. database modeling
   C. normalization   D. decomposition

6. In an operating system, a situation occurs in which one process is in a   6.____
   waiting queue on another process that is also waiting on another process and
   the last one is waiting on the first process so no process is progressing in this
   waiting circular. This is called
   A. deadlock   B. starvation
   C. dormant   D. none of the above

7. Which access control method is considered the BEST approach for   7.____
   restricting system access to authorized users?
   A. Role-based access control   B. Process-based access control
   C. Job-based access control   D. None of the above

8. Which of the following is a disadvantage of a distributed system?   8.____
   A. Incremental growth   B. Reliability
   C. Resource sharing   D. All of the above

9. Which of the following is the BEST example of batch processing?   9.____
   A. Video game control   B. Online reservation system
   C. Preparing pay bills of employees   D. None of the above

10. Which of the following techniques was initiated to keep both CPU and the   10.____
    I/O devices busy because it was not possible with the single job?
    A. Time-sharing   B. Spooling
    C. Preemptive scheduling   D. Multiprogramming

11. Distributed operating system is based on the principle of   11.____
    A. single system image   B. multi-system image
    C. wireless networks   D. none of the above

12. The following components are helpful in a successful database environment   12.____
    EXCEPT
    A. users   B. database
    C. separate files   D. database administrator

13. In DBMS, which of the following is NOT schema?   13.____
    A. Database schema   B. Logical schema
    C. None of the above

14. Of the following, which SQL Query is used to remove the table and all its   14.____
    data from the database?
    A. Drop table   B. Delete table
    C. Alter table   D. None of the above

15. *Ellipses* in DBMS means   15.____
    A. weak entity set   B. attributes
    C. primary key   D. none of the above

16. The method which performs a set of union of two "similarly structured"   16.____
    tables is called
    A. union   B. join
    C. addition   D. none of the above

17. All details about the files, its ownership, permissions, and location of file 17.____
    contents are stored in
    A. file control block (FCB)   B. computer history
    C. file system   D. none of the above

18. The drawback of a file management system to store data is   18.____
    A. data redundancy and inconstancy
    B. difficulty in accessing data
    C. data isolation
    D. all of the above

19. Which of the following is a feature of the machine independent operating
    system?
    A. Management of real time memory   B. File processing
    C. I/O supervision   D. Job scheduling
    E. B and D   F. A and C

19.____

20. As a computer support officer, you are given details for your company's customers,
    consisting of two lists of names and addresses. You need to produce it in an
    individual document that consists of both names and address list. For this
    purpose, which mail merge would you prefer?
    A. Main document   B. Data source
    C. Mail merge   D. Merge field

20.____

21. After once creating a customer list with mail merge, which button will help
    you to add, delete or update your customer list?
    A. *Data Source* button   B. *Edit* button
    C. *Edit Data Source* button D. *Data Editing* button

21.____

22. Which of the following steps is NOT a part of the three basic *Mail Merge
    Helper* steps?
    A. Merge the two files   B. Create the main document
    C. Set the mailing list parameters D. Create the data source

22.____

23. As a computer support officer, while completing your assigned document
    typed in MS Word 2013, you need to insert the page number in the footer, but
    when you click on the insert tab > footer, it appears as *1*, but you wish to show *i*
    (roman numbers). What procedure will be followed?
    A. From Home, select bullets and numbering and configure the necessary
       setting
    B. From Insert Tab, choose Page Number and specify necessary setting
    C. Click on Page Number Icon and select Format Page Number and specify
       required setting
    D. All of the above

23.____

24. The problem statement contains the _____, which consists of these lists:
    I.   Lists specific input programs
    II.   Precise output values
    III. Perfect program would return for those input values

    A. Testing plan   B. Error handler
    C. Requirement list   D. Input-output specification

24.____

25. As a computer support officer who knows the stages of team development
    that will lead this team to a winning combination, what are the stages in proper
    sequence?
    A. Forming, storming, norming and performing
    B. Forming, norming, performing and finalizing
    C. Forming, storming, norming and playing
    D. None of the above

25.____

KEY (CORRECT ANSWERS)

1.	B		11.	B
2.	C		12.	C
3.	A		13.	B
4.	C		14.	C
5.	C		15.	B
6.	A		16.	A
7.	A		17.	A
8.	B		18.	D
9.	C		19.	E
10.	D		20.	C

21.	C
22.	C
23.	C
24.	A
25.	A

———————

TEST 4

DIRECTIONS: Each question or incomplete statement is followed by several suggested answers or completions. Select the one that BEST answers the question or completes the statement. *PRINT THE LETTER OF THE CORRECT ANSWER IN THE SPACE AT THE RIGHT.*

1. Data users are those who   1._____
   A. use data for their own advantage, breaking the law
   B. store files and data for their specific purposes
   C. use the data in databases
   D. none of the above

2. Which type of chart would be the BEST choice for showing how the   2._____
   temperature of a pizza changes over time when it is put in the oven?
   A. Pie chart   B. Line graph
   C. Bar chart   D. None of the above

3. As a computer support officer, you have to continuously update and   3._____
   organize your directories, folders and files on your computer. Which of the
   following BEST suits your requirement?
   A. Microsoft Word   B. Any spreadsheet application
   C. Windows Explorer   D. Microsoft Internet Explorer

4. Upgrade installation means   4._____
   A. preparation for installation, installation itself, any required or optional
      steps following the installation
   B. completely formatting the operating system on hardware and install new
      software
   C. type of system installation on a computer that already has an earlier
      version of the operating system
   D. none of the above

5. The main job of an operating system is   5._____
   A. command resources   B. manage resources
   C. provide utilities   D. none of the above

6. The MOST common source of change data in refreshing a data warehouse   6._____
   is _____ change data.
   A. queryable   B. cooperative   C. logged   D. snapshot

7. Which of the following is NOT an advantage of multiprogramming?   7._____
   A. Increased throughput
   B. Shorter response time
   C. Decreased operating system overhead
   D. Ability to assign priorities to jobs

8. In ERD, the rectangles are divided into two parts that show   8.____
     A. entity set   B. relationship set
     C. set of attributes   D. primary key

9. The MAXIMUM numbers of entities that can be participating in a relationship   9.____
are designed with
     A. minimum cardinality   B. maximum cardinality
     C. entity relation diagram   D. none of the above

10. Which of the following is a multi-valued attribute?   10.____
     A. Phone number   B. Name
     C. Date of birth   D. Place of birth
     E. None of the above

11. Which term is used to refer to a specific record in your medicine database;   11.____
for instance, information stored about a specific illness?
     A. Relation   B. Instance
     C. Table   D. None of the above

12. The relation stud (ID, name, house no., credit, house no., city, department)   12.____
is decomposed into stud1 (ID, name) stud2 (name, house no., city,
department). This type of decomposition is called
     A. lossless decomposition   B. lossless-join decomposition
     C. both A and B   D. none of the above

13. As a technical support officer for a large organization, you have to ensure   13.____
the uninterrupted availability of data by creating backup to deal with every
possible data loss. Backup is taken by
     A. erasing all previous records and creating new records
     B. sending all log records from primary site to the remote backup site
     C. sending only selected records from main site to the alternate site
     D. none of the above

14. Verbal exchange of information between parents and a school staff when a   14.____
student is moved from one department to another is a report which includes
necessary information to maintain a consistent support for students of one
department to another. This report is known as a
     A. transfer report   B. hand-off report
     C. graphic record   D. report

15. Which portable storage device would you prefer for backups or showing   15.____
your photographs to your friend?
     A. USB stick   B. Hard drive
     C. Joystick   D. None of the above

16. Which is the exact step for problem solving?   16.____
    A. Observe, evaluate and adjust
    B. Collect and analyze data
    C. Identify and analyze the problem
    D. Consider possible solutions

17. The software that maintains the time of a microprocessor to assure that   17.____
    all time critical events are processed as efficiently as possible and also system
    activities are divided into independent tasks is known as
    A. shell processor   B. kernel
    C. device driver   D. none of the above

18. Which of the following is the MOST appropriate scheduling technique in   18.____
    real time operating systems?
    A. Round robin   B. FCFS
    C. Pre-emptive scheduling   D. Random scheduling

19. Use case diagrams consist of   19.____
    A. actor   B. prototype
    C. none of the above   D. all of the above

20. Data warehouse means   20.____
    A. the actual directory of a knowledge
    B. the stage of selecting the right data for a KDD process
    C. a subject-oriented integrated time variant non-volatile collection of data in
       support of management
    D. all of the above

21. Jane wants to advertise her home-based bakery. For this purpose she needs   21.____
    to develop a two-column promotion for the daily local newspaper. She selected
    MS Word for this purpose, but does not know exactly which option to use. Of
    the following, what would you suggest she use for newspaper style columns?
    A. Insert Tab > Smart Art   B. Table > Insert Table
    C. Insert Tab > Textbox   D. Page Layout Tab > Columns

22. Of the following, what would you suggest Jane in Question 21 use to add   22.____
    Shimmer and Sparkle text in her advertisement to make it more attractive and
    eye capturing?
    A. Word Art   B. Font styles
    C. Text effects   D. Font effects

23. In MS Word, which indent marker is specific to control all the lines excluding   23.____
    the first line?
    A. First Line Indent Marker   B. Left Indent Marker
    C. Hanging Indent Marker   D. Right Indent Marker

24. When working as a computer support officer, you receive a help call from one of the users. The problem is that the user has just deleted an entire folder of important office notes. He needs to retrieve the data. Which method would you adopt to retrieve the contents?
    A. Empty the recycle bin
    B. Restore the folder from the recycle bin
    C. Once deleted, its contents cannot be retrieved
    D. No need to worry. Only the folder has been deleted, not its contents.

24._____

25. Documentation can be explained as
    A. a procedure used to provide technical information to specific audiences who have specific needs for that information
    B. an explanation about all procedures and their mechanisms
    C. a method that specifies the author, source and related detail about information
    D. none of the above

25._____

KEY (CORRECT ANSWERS)

1.	B		11.	A
2.	B		12.	D
3.	C		13.	B
4.	C		14.	A
5.	B		15.	A
6.	E		16.	C
7.	C		17.	B
8.	A		18.	C
9.	B		19.	D
10.	A		20.	C

21.	D
22.	D
23.	B
24.	B
25.	C

EXAMINATION SECTION
TEST 1

DIRECTIONS: Each question or incomplete statement is followed by several suggested answers or completions. Select the one the BEST answers the question or completes the statement. *PRINT THE LETTER OF THE CORRECT ANSWER IN THE SPACE AT THE RIGHT.*

1. Which of the following was an advantage associated with open source software in the 1990s?   1._____

   A. A standard user interface for productivity applications such as word processing and spreadsheets
   B. Stringent quality control processes
   C. Suitability for mission-critical applications
   D. A broadened community of programmers who can stabilize and add functionality to software

2. IP addresses   2._____
   I. are attached to every node on the Internet
   II. are sometimes listed as a character string
   III. establish a direct link between sender and recipient
   IV. use circuit-switching technology

   A. I only
   B. I and II
   C. II, III and IV
   D. I, II, III and IV

3. Programming languages used exclusively for artificial intelligence applications include   3._____

   A. AIML and Prolog
   B. LISP and Prolog
   C. Ada and LISP
   D. Delphi and Python

4. Cookies are usually stored by browsers as   4._____

   A. text files
   B. algorithms
   C. tokens
   D. HTML files

5. Analysts typically use each of the following to evaluate the flow of data through an information system, EXCEPT   5._____

   A. decision trees
   B. Gantt charts
   C. structured English
   D. data flow diagrams

6. Methods for protecting a computer system from viruses include   6._____
   I. accessing a Web site that offers on-line virus scans

II. checking physical media, such as floppy disks or DVDs, before they are used in a computer
III. erecting a firewall
IV. never opening e-mail attachments from people unknown to the user

A. I and IV
B. II, III and IV
C. III and IV only
D. I, II, III and IV

7. Describing an algorithm as "general" means that it

A. does not have a clear stopping point
B. addresses the stated problem in all instances
C. can be carried out in any sequence
D. can be expressed in any language

7.____

8. Packet-switching offers each of the following advantages, EXCEPT

A. faster transmission of data
B. greater network user capacity
C. greater degree of redundancy
D. more localized data corruption

8.____

9. The term "digital divide" describes the discrepancies between

A. people who have access to, and the resources to use, new information and communication technologies, and people who do not
B. approximations in the values of floating-point numbers by a processor
C. the rate at which computer processing speeds increase and the rate at which the capacity to store data increases
D. data that is entered into a database application and the information that is displayed to an end-user

9.____

10. The main advantage of using programmable microcode is that

A. programs can be made very small and portable
B. the CPU's capacity is never overclocked
C. the same instructions can be executed on different hardware platforms
D. it is usually executed more quickly than other program code

10.____

11. Cache memory is NOT

A. used only in large computers
B. used to solve the problem of inadequate primary memory
C. divided into the two main categories of RAM cache and secondary cache
D. used to improve processing speed

11.____

12. When PC users ask for a document to be sent to them, they should request a .txt file, because it

A. comes with a built-in antivirus program
B. will only transmit text

12.____

C.   denotes a disinfected file
D.   cannot contain malicious and executable code

13. Line personnel in an organization can enter transaction data and see totals and other   13.____
    results immediately by use of _____ processing

    A.   summary
    B.   batch
    C.   on-line
    D.   real-time

14. A network with a main computer that does all of the processing for a number of simple   14.____
    display units is described as

    A.   peer-to-peer
    B.   client-file server
    C.   n-tier
    D.   terminal emulation

15. All buses consist of two parts, the _____ bus and the _____ bus.   15.____

    A.   internal; external
    B.   main; expansion
    C.   ISA; PCI
    D.   address; data

16. The _____ is a small amount of high-speed memory thatstores regularly used data.   16.____

    A.   cache
    B.   spool
    C.   buffer
    D.   frame

17. Technological cornerstones of the Internet include each of the following, EXCEPT   17.____

    A.   HTML
    B.   TCP/IP
    C.   URL
    D.   MMDS

18. The OSI (Open System Interconnection) model defines a networking framework for   18.____
    implementing protocols in seven layers. The _____ layer, or layer 3, provides switching
    and routing technologies, creating logical paths, known as virtual circuits, for transmitting
    data from node to node

    A.   network
    B.   presentation
    C.   transport
    D.   session

19. The main difference between the Windows NT operating system and the current Windows OS is that the NT operating system   19.____

    A.   has no relationship to MS-DOS
    B.   has a different user interface
    C.   runs faster
    D.   supports more peripheral devices

20. Before sound can be handled on a computer, it must first be converted to electrical energy, and then transformed through an analog-to-digital converter into a digital representation. _____ Law states that the more often a sound wave is sampled, the more accurate the digital representation.   20.____

    A.   Gilder's
    B.   Moore's
    C.   Amdahl's
    D.   Nyquist's

21. The primary disadvantage associated with interpreted programming languages, such as Java, is that they   21.____

    A.   present fewer solutions to individual problems
    B.   have slower execution speeds
    C.   are not as portable
    D.   are more difficult for programmers to understand

22. The advantages promised by the emerging technology of holographic storage include   22.____
    I.   higher storage densities
    II.   easier synchronization with the CPU
    III.   non-volatility
    IV.   faster data transfer speeds

    A.   I only
    B.   I and IV
    C.   II and III
    D.   III and IV

23. A file that contains instructions in a particular computer's machine language is said to contain _____ code.   23.____

    A.   macro
    B.   object
    C.   scripting
    D.   source

24. A computer uses _____ to transform raw data into useful information.   24.____

    A.   input devices and output devices
    B.   a processor and memory
    C.   memory and a motherboard
    D.   language and protocols

5 (#1)

25. In computer graphics, the term "raster graphics" is synonymous with   25._____

    A. vector graphics
    B. bitmapped graphics
    C. object-oriented graphics
    D. autosizing

26. In 1996, journalist and former White House Press Secretary Pierre Salinger, making a   26._____
    public statement about the causes of the recent TWA Flight 800 crash, became the fig-
    urehead for what is now known as the "Pierre Salinger Syndrome" This phenomenon
    refers to the

    A. act of hiding information by embedding messages within another
    B. pit those who have the skills, knowledge and abilities to use the technologies
       against those who do not
    C. tendency to believe that everything one reads on the Internet is true
    D. practice of using software to monitor the behavior of a user visiting a Web site or
       sending an e-mail

27. Which of the following is NOT a term that is interchangeable with "expansion card"?   27._____

    A. Expansion file
    B. Expansion board
    C. Adapter
    D. Socket

28. Multidimensional database management systems are also referred to as   28._____

    A. Relational database management systems
    B. On-line Transaction Processing (OLTP)
    C. SQL servers
    D. On-line Analytical Processing (OLAP)

29. The primary difference between "smart" and "dumb" printers is that   29._____

    A. smart printers can perform dithering
    B. smart printers use a page description language
    C. dumb printers use less system memory
    D. dumb printers cannot bitmap vector graphics

30. The interface between the CPU and the hard disk's electronics is known as the hard disk   30._____

    A. navigator
    B. manager
    C. reticulate
    D. controller

31. A single _____ port can be used to connect as many as 127 peripheral devices to a   31._____
    computer.

    A. PIA
    B. Fire Wire
    C. parallel
    D. USB

32. In the binary system, 1011 equals a decimal   32.____

    A. 2
    B. 3
    C. 11
    D. 12

33. A transistor radio is an example of _____ transmission of data   33.____

    A. half-duplex
    B. full-duplex
    C. half-simplex
    D. simplex

34. Which of the following is NOT a type of liquid crystal display?   34.____

    A. Active matrix
    B. Passive matrix
    C. Electroluminescent
    D. Dual-scan

35. Which of the following is a term for commercial software that has been pirated and made   35.____
available to the public via a bulletin board system (BBS) or the Internet?

    A. Freeware
    B. Crackware
    C. Warez
    D. Shareware

36. IBM-compatible PCs denote the primary hard disk with the   36.____

    A. number 1
    B. letter A
    C. letter C
    D. letter X

37. Each of the following operating systems provides some kind of graphical user interface,   37.____
EXCEPT

    A. Macintosh OS
    B. Linux
    C. UNIX
    D. DOS

38. An operating system's overall quality is most often judged on its ability to manage   38.____

    A. program execution
    B. device drivers
    C. disk utilities
    D. application backup

39. In multimedia product development, elements of a program are arranged into separate   39.____

    A. tracks
    B. columns

C. zones
D. layers

40. The CPU contains the _____ unit.   40.____
    I.   I/O
    II. control
    III. arithmetic
    IV. instructing decoding

    A. I and II
    B. I, II and IV
    C. II and V
    D. I, II, III and IV

41. The on-line application that locates and displays the document associated with a hyper-   41.____
    link is a(n)

    A. server
    B. plug-in
    C. browser
    D. finder

42. Which of the following devices requires a driver?   42.____
    I.   printer
    II. mouse
    III. DVD drive
    IV. keyboard

    A. I only
    B. I, II and IV
    C. II and IV
    D. I,II, III and IV

43. Database management systems include each of the following components, EXCEPT   43.____

    A. data collection applications
    B. statistical analysis applications
    C. data modification applications
    D. query languages

44. Waves are characterized by each of the following, EXCEPT   44.____

    A. Frequency
    B. Pulse
    C. Frequency
    D. Amplitude

45. Although considered to be outdated by many programmers, _____ is still the most   45.____
    widely used programming language in the world.

    A. Pascal
    B. COBOL
    C. FORTRAN
    D. BASIC

46. A graphics program using the _____ model represents three-dimensional objects by displaying their outlines and edges.   46._____

   A. wireframe
   B. volumetric
   C. solid
   D. surface

47. The concept central to the legislation that regulates telephone service in the United States is   47._____

   A. broadband service
   B. consumer price parity
   C. reasonable access time
   D. universal access

48. In order to be certified as "open source" by the Open Source Institute (OSI), a program must meet each of the following criteria, EXCEPT that the   48._____

   A. rights attached to the program are contingent on the program's being part of a particular software distribution
   B. author or holder of the license of the source code cannot collect royalties on the distribution of the program
   C. distributed program must make the source code accessible to the user
   D. licensed software cannot place restrictions on other software distributed with it

49. Ethernet systems typically use a _____ topology.   49._____

   A. bus
   B. star
   C. ring
   D. tree

50. In enterprises, the _____ is the computer that routes the traffic from a workstation to the outside network that is serving the Web pages.   50._____

   A. proxy server
   B. ISP
   C. packet switcher
   D. gateway

KEY (CORRECT ANSWERS)

1. D	11. A	21. B	31. D	41. C
2. B	12. D	22. B	32. C	42. D
3. B	13. C	23. B	33. D	43. A
4. A	14. A	24. B	34. C	44. B
5. B	15. D	25. B	35. C	45. B
6. D	16. A	26. C	36. C	46. A
7. B	17. D	27. D	37. D	47. D
8. A	18. A	28. D	38. A	48. A
9. A	19. A	29. B	39. A	49. A
10. C	20. D	30. D	40. B	50. D

TEST 2

DIRECTIONS: Each question or incomplete statement is followed by several suggested answers or completions. Select the one the BEST answers the question or completes the statement. *PRINT THE LETTER OF THE CORRECT ANSWER IN THE SPACE AT THE RIGHT.*

1. "Refresh rate" typically refers to the

    A. number of times RAM is updated in a second
    B. time it takes to completely rewrite a disk
    C. number of times the display monitor is redrawn in a second
    D. time it takes for a Web pages to reload

1.____

2. In a markup language, authors use _____ to identify portions of a document.

    A. icons
    B. schemas
    C. numbers
    D. elements

2.____

3. Object-oriented programming languages rely heavily on _____ to create high-level objects.

    I. formalization
    II. abstraction
    III. information hiding
    IV. encapsulation

    A. I only
    B. I, II and III
    C. II, III and IV
    D. I, II, III and IV

3.____

4. The base unit of three-dimensional graphics is the

    A. texel
    B. voxel
    C. pixel
    D. bit

4.____

5. In computing, "gamma correction" typically refers to an adjustment in the

    A. light intensity of a scanner, monitor, or printer
    B. amplitude modulation
    C. emission of gamma waves by a CRT monitor
    D. speed with which analog data is digitized

5.____

6. The OSI (Open System Interconnection) model defines a networking framework for implementing protocols in seven layers. The seventh layer of the OSI model consists of the

    A. hardware
    B. applications

6.____

C. protocols
D. network

7. A significant difference between frame switching packet switching is that frame switching   7._____

    A. offers accelerated packet processing
    B. creates a virtual circuit
    C. allows multiple connections on the same set of hardware
    D. contains now quality-of-service assurances

8. In _____ memory, each location has an actual "address."   8._____

    A. RAM
    B. ROM
    C. PROM
    D. EPROM

9. Video applications require a bare minimum of _____ frames per second in order to   9._____
function.

    A. 8
    B. 15
    C. 30
    D. 60

10. The most commonly used network application today is   10._____

    A. Web design
    B. BBS
    C. e-mail
    D. software downloading

11. Standardized codes for representing character data numerically include   11._____
    I. ANSI
    II. EBCDIC
    III. ASCII
    IV. DECS

    A. I and II
    B. II and III
    C. II, III and IV
    D. I, II, III and IV

12. Photolithography is the process of transferring geometric shapes on a mask to the sur-   12._____
face of a silicon wafer. Possible future alternative technologies to photolithography
include each of the following, EXCEPT the

    A. multiple-wave laser beam
    B. electron beam
    C. extreme ultraviolet
    D. X-ray

13. Hard disk mechanisms typically contain a single   13.____

    A. head actuator
    B. read/write head
    C. platter
    D. landing zone

14. Contemporary Rapid Application Development (RAD) emphasizes the reduction of   14.____
development time through

    A. trimming code
    B. inserting pre-written artificial intelligence capabilities
    C. establishing a graphical user interface
    D. making slight modifications to proprietary software

15. A Web site contains a number of databases that contain all the information about an   15.____
organization's clients-such as names, addresses, credit card information, past invoices,
etc.). This is an example of a data

    A. mine
    B. warehouse
    C. dictionary
    D. mart

16. Currently, a computer's most difficult task would be to   16.____

    A. speak in long paragraphs
    B. recognize spoken words
    C. interpret the meaning of words
    D. compose a syntactically correct item of discourse

17. An API is a(n)   17.____

    A. algorithm for the lossless compression of files
    B. set of routines, protocols, and tools for building software applications
    C. piece of software that helps the operating system communicate with a peripheral
       device
    D. code for representing characters as numbers

18. The disadvantages associated with ring LAN topologies include   18.____
      I. more limited geographical range
      II. low bandwidth
      III. high expense
      IV. complex and difficult installation

    A. I only
    B. I and II
    C. III and IV
    D. I, II, III and IV

19. Scientists would most likely use _____ to analyze variations in planetary orbits.   19.____

    A. a mainframe
    B. the Internet

C. a supercomputer
D. a virtual network

20. The primary disadvantage to shared-memory multiprocessing involves   20._____

    A. slow retrieval speeds
    B. bus overload
    C. inadequate trace width
    D. RAM purges

21. If a computer user enters a legal command that does not make any sense in the given   21._____
    context, the user has committed an error of

    A. syntax
    B. semantics
    C. formatting
    D. parsing

22. Which of the following terms is NOT synonymous with the others?   22._____

    A. Floating point unit
    B. Numeric coprocessor
    C. Math coprocessor
    D. Accelerator board

23. Which of the following is a measure of data transfer capacity?   23._____

    A. Duplication rate
    B. Bandwidth
    C. Frequency
    D. Baud rate

24. In the 1990s, the main obstacle to the use of the Linux operating system in desktop appli-   24._____
    cations was

    A. the lack of a standard user interface
    B. difficulties in file and print serving
    C. inability to accommodate multiple platforms
    D. insufficient support from the commercial sector

25. Which of the following external bus standards supports "hot plugging"–the ability to add   25._____
    and remove devices to a computer while the computer is running and have the operating
    system automatically recognize the change?

    A. Serial
    B. USB
    C. PCI
    D. Parallel port

26. When a key on a computer keyboard is struck, each of the following may occur, EXCEPT   26._____

    A. a cursor on the screen moves
    B. a scan code is sent to an application

C. a binary number is input into the computer
D. an EBCDIC code for a letter is sent to a word processing application

27. SONET 27.____

A. cannot be used to link digital networks to fiber optics
B. is a synchronous Layer 1 protocol
C. prohibits data streams of different speeds from being multiplexed in the same line
D. can scale up to 4 Gbps

28. A user handles data stored on a disk with the utility program known as the 28.____

A. file sorter
B. file manager
C. disk scanner
D. finder

29. A _____ is a tool that helps users of word processing or desktop publishing applications 29.____
to avoid formatting complex documents individually.

A. merge
B. column
C. template
D. table

30. Which of the following is a high-level programming language that is particularly suited for 30.____
use on the World Wide Web, often through the use of small, downloadable applications
known as applets?

A. XML
B. Ada
C. Java
D. C++

31. Microprocessor speeds have increased dramatically over the past two decades, largely 31.____
as a result of significant

A. improvements in hardware breakpoints
B. increases in trace depth
C. compression of overlay RAM
D. reductions in trace width

32. On most PCs, this contains all the code required to control the keyboard, display screen, 32.____
disk drives, serial communications, and a number of miscellaneous functions.

A. Flash memory
B. Operating system
C. BIOS
D. USB

33. Which of the following is a rating system originally designed to help parents and teachers   33.____
control what children access on the Internet, but now also used to facilitate other uses for
labels, including code signing and privacy?

    A. V-chip
    B. Recreational Software Advisory Council
    C. Platform for Internet Content Selection
    D. Cyber Patrol

34. A database designed for continuous addition and deletion of records is said to perform   34.____
the function of _____ processing.

    A. batch
    B. drilldown
    C. transaction
    D. analytical

35. A unique 128-bit number, produced by the Windows OS or by some Windows applica-   35.____
tions to identify a particular component, application, file, database entry, and/or user is
known as a

    A. key
    B. GUID
    C. PGP
    D. DLL

36. Compared to private-key cryptograph, public-key   36.____

    A. uses two keys
    B. is easier to understand
    C. functions more smoothly with contemporary networks
    D. requires fewer computations

37. Static RAM (SRAM) is used to   37.____

    A. supplement the main memory
    B. determine which information should be kept in the cache
    C. form the memory cache
    D. form the disk cache

38. A(n) _____ system is used to produce reports that will help managers throughout an   38.____
organization to evaluate their departments.

    A. expert
    B. management information
    C. office automation
    D. transaction processing

39. Software that may be delivered/downloaded and used without charge, but is neverthe-   39.____
less still copyrighted by the author, is known as

    A. public-domain software
    B. shareware

C. open-source software
D. freeware

40. Barriers to widespread use of cable modems in Internet access include   40.____
    I.   the one-way transmission design of the television infrastructure
    II. uncertain capacity of television infrastructure
    III. complexity of protocols
    IV. bandwidth restrictions

A. I only
B. I and II
C. II and IV
D. I, II, III and IV

41. Which of the following is NOT a function that can be performed with a spreadsheet appli-   41.____
cation?

A. Budget charts and graphs
B. Inventory management
C. Audiovisual presentations
D. Fiscal forecasting

42. Which of the following is a Windows-based graphical user interface for the UNIX operat-   42.____
ing system?

A. Linux
B. Gnu
C. MOTIF
D. UNI

43. In a database, the _____ contains a code, number, name, or some other information   43.____
that uniquely identifies the record.

A. primary key
B. file
C. schema
D. key field

44. Which of the following terms is NOT synonymous with the others?   44.____

A. Web bug
B. Clear GIF
C. Web beacon
D. Cookie

45. As a firewall technology, the proxy server operates by   45.____

A. examining each packet that enters or exits a network, and accepts or rejects it
based on a given set of rules
B. applying security mechanisms to specific applications
C. constantly changing its location
D. intercepting all messages entering and leaving a network

46. VRAM is a specific kind of memory used to   46.____

    A. accelerate processing speeds
    B. store video display data
    C. create virtual addresses, rather than real addresses, to store data and instructions
    D. create a virtual environment for the user

47. Which phase of the application development process serves to identify features that   47.____
must be added to the program to make it satisfactory to users?

    A. Software concept
    B. Coding and debugging
    C. System testing
    D. Requirements analysis

48. What is the term for the natural data size of a computer?   48.____

    A. Word size
    B. Clock speed
    C. Bus width
    D. Cache

49. Microkernels operate by moving many of the operating system services into "user space"   49.____
that other operating systems keep in the kernel. This migration tends to have each of the
following effects, EXCEPT greater

    A. security
    B. bug immunity for the kernel
    C. configurability
    D. "fixed" memory footprint

50. High-level programming languages are   50.____
    I.   useful when speed is essential
    II. processor-independent
    III. usually compiled or assembled
    IV. easier to read, write and maintain than other languages

    A. I and IV
    B. I, II, and III
    C. II, III and IV
    D. I, II, III and IV

KEY (CORRECT ANSWERS)

1.	C	11.	C	21.	B	31.	D	41.	C
2.	D	12.	A	22.	D	32.	C	42.	C
3.	C	13.	A	23.	B	33.	C	43.	A
4.	A	14.	C	24.	A	34.	C	44.	D
5.	A	15.	B	25.	B	35.	B	45.	D
6.	B	16.	C	26.	D	36.	A	46.	B
7.	B	17.	B	27.	B	37.	C	47.	C
8.	A	18.	C	28.	B	38.	B	48.	A
9.	B	19.	C	29.	C	39.	C	49.	D
10.	C	20.	B	30.	C	40.	B	50.	C

EXAMINATION SECTION
TEST 1

DIRECTIONS: Each question or incomplete statement is followed by several suggested
answers or completions. Select the one the BEST answers the question or
completes the statement. *PRINT THE LETTER OF THE CORRECT ANSWER
IN THE SPACE AT THE RIGHT.*

1. Which of the following types of firewall techniques is most susceptible to IP spoofing?   1.____

    A. Proxy server
    B. Circuit-level gateway
    C. Packet filter
    D. Application gateway

2. Which of the following is a term for unorganized symbols, words, images, numbers or   2.____
sound that a computer can transform into something useful?

    A. Software
    B. Data
    C. Input
    D. Information

3. In relational databases, records are referred to as   3.____

    A. stories
    B. tuples
    C. keys
    D. files

4. Web _____ can be included in HTML-formatted e-mail messages to reveal whether a   4.____
recipient has received a message, as well as to disclose the recipient's IP address.

    A. cookies
    B. bots
    C. bugs
    D. tokens

5. Which of the following is NOT typically an element of a GUI?   5.____

    A. Column
    B. Icon
    C. Pointer
    D. Menu

6. Of the three general methods for posing queries to a database, choosing parameters   6.____
from a menu

    A. is the least flexible
    B. is the most powerful
    C. requires the user to learn a specialized language
    D. presents the user with a blank record and lets him/her specify fields and values

7. Unless the circuitry is part of a workstation's design, LAN computers usually need a(n) _____ to function in the network.

    7._____

    A. NIC
    B. bus
    C. protocol
    D. EDI

8. A VPN enables a business to

    8._____

    A. avoid network "tear-downs"
    B. make use of the Internet, rather than build a dedicated network
    C. make a network inherently more secure
    D. work on circuits, rather than packets

9. In a client/server architecture, the component that performs the bulk of the data processing operations is known as the

    9._____

    A. fat client
    B. portal
    C. server
    D. node

10. The process of translating virtual addresses into real addresses is known as

    10._____

    A. paging
    B. ghosting
    C. mapping
    D. swapping

11. The first commercially developed operating system was

    11._____

    A. OS1
    B. Windows
    C. OS360
    D. DOS

12. The relationships between cells in a spreadsheet application are known as

    12._____

    A. formulas
    B. references
    C. attributes
    D. labels

13. Most contemporary personal computers come with external cache memory that sits between the CPU and the main memory. This cache is known as the _____ cache.

    13._____

    A. disk
    B. DRAM
    C. Level 1 (L1)
    D. Level 2 (L2)

14. Only _____ language programs can manipulate CPU registers.   14.____
    I.   machine
    II. assembly
    III. high-level
    IV. fourth-generation

    A. I and II
    B. II only
    C. I, II and III
    D. IV only

15. In the _____ process, the amplitude of an analog wave is checked at regular intervals in   15.____
order to enable its encoding into digital form.

    A. attenuation
    B. sampling
    C. amplification
    D. modulation

16. In the _____ phase of the systems development life cycle, programmers either write   16.____
software from scratch or purchase software from a vendor.

    A. implementation
    B. maintenance
    C. needs analysis
    D. development

17. The term "warm boot" refers to   17.____

    A. getting a quick view of stored files
    B. placing files in a more secure location
    C. restarting a computer that is already on
    D. making files more quickly available on a disk

18. In terms of digital security, nonrepudiation can be accomplished through each of the fol-   18.____
lowing, EXCEPT

    A. confirmation services
    B. timestamps
    C. nym servers
    D. digital signatures

19. More advanced microprocessors may begin executing a second instruction before the   19.____
first has been complete. This is a feature known as

    A. multitasking
    B. burst mode
    C. pipelining
    D. cascading

20. The main disadvantage associated with ATM network technology is that it   20.____

    A. tends to favor audio and video over traditional data
    B. creates cells of unpredictable size
    C. does not respond well to fluctuations in network traffic
    D. requires large startup costs

21. Computer users make use of hypertext in browser software by clicking the mouse on a   21.____

    A. graphic image
    B. pull-down menu choice
    C. hot spot
    D. button

22. Products using the IEEE 1394 interface may use each of the following names, EXCEPT   22.____

    A. i.link
    B. USB
    C. Fire Wire
    D. Lynx

23. What is the term for the computer's processing circuitry, located within the system's case?   23.____

    A. CPU
    B. RAM
    C. Motherboard
    D. BIOS

24. The primary difficulty in using a LAN to directly connect telephone calls to a server is that   24.____

    A. it would prevent the LAN from working with another remote network
    B. the configuration of the network would change into something that could not strictly be considered a "LAN"
    C. most LAN technologies don't handle voice data very well
    D. the link would require synchronous data

25. Graphical software developers can create virtual environments from two-dimensional images by making use of   25.____

    A. Quicktime VR
    B. MPEG
    C. transcoding
    D. Cinepak

26. In the design of an information system, a(n) _____ is often useful to show all organizations, departments, users, applications, and data that function in the system.   26.____

    A. Gantt chart
    B. data dictionary
    C. schema
    D. entity-relationship diagram

27. Which of the following terms is NOT synonymous with the others? 27.____

    A. Bit rate
    B. Vertical frequency
    C. Refresh rate
    D. Frame rate

28. What is the term for the process of adding depth to an image using a volumetric dataset (a set of cross-sectional images)? 28.____

    A. Voxelization
    B. Texelization
    C. Interpixellation
    D. Rounding out

29. Assembly language must be translated into _____ before it can run on a computer. 29.____

    A. source code
    B. pseudocode
    C. machine language
    D. BASIC

30. Indexing a database field offers the benefit of 30.____

    A. establishing an encryption code for selected data items
    B. allowing for the programming of an interface
    C. duplicating information contained within the field for backup purposes
    D. accelerating searches in that field

31. Some computer keyboards have a(n) _____ integrated into them, between the g and h keys. 31.____

    A. mini-mouse
    B. trackball
    C. light pen
    D. integrated pointing device

32. Which of the following is a 16-bit standard for denoting characters that can represent most of the world's languages? 32.____

    A. ANSI
    B. ASCII
    C. Unicode
    D. ISO Latin-1

33. Mosaic is a _____ browser. 33.____

    A. graphical
    B. text-only
    C. markup
    D. plug-in

34. Which of the following can be used to enhance the performance of executing commands on a database? 34.____

    A. Connection pools
    B. Two-phase commits
    C. Fixed lengths
    D. Triggers

35. The FIRST step in the photolithographic process is 35.____

    A. soft baking
    B. wafer cleaning
    C. barrier layer formation
    D. mask alignment

36. Computer program instructions 36.____
    I. are explicit and unequivocal
    II. perform only one task each
    III. are translated into binary code before execution
    IV. are executed in sequence

    A. I and II
    B. I, II and III
    C. III and IV
    D. I, II, III and IV

37. When transferred to a different computer, a(n) _____ language requires very little repro- 37.____
gramming.

    A. high-level
    B. machine
    C. assembly
    D. natural

38. Typically, the operating system kernel is responsible for managing each of the following, 38.____
EXCEPT

    A. peripherals
    B. program execution
    C. memory
    D. disk

39. The UNIX operating system was the first major program written in the computer lan- 39.____
guage

    A. Ada
    B. C
    C. Java
    D. C++

40. The _____ version of a software product is given to manufacturers to bundle into future versions of their hardware products.

    40.____

    A. alpha
    B. maintenance
    C. crippled
    D. RTM

41. MOUS is an acronym that stands for

    41.____

    A. Memory Overload/Unusable System
    B. Modulation User Set
    C. Microsoft Office Utility Service
    D. Microsoft Office User Specialist

42. The opposite of "time sharing" in microprocessing is

    42.____

    A. multitasking
    B. autosizing
    C. multiprocessing
    D. batch processing

43. A standard compact disc can contain about _____ MB of data.

    43.____

    A. 480
    B. 650
    C. 720
    D. 800

44. Which of the following is LEAST similar to the others in its function?

    44.____

    A. Extension
    B. Command file
    C. Script
    D. Macro

45. Tools for analyzing data in spreadsheet programs include each of the following, EXCEPT

    45.____

    A. conceptual problem-solving
    B. risk modeling
    C. sensitivity analysis
    D. goal seeking

46. Many optical scanners are capable of gray scaling, and typically use from _____ different shades of gray.

    46.____

    A. 8 to 32
    B. 16 to 256
    C. 512 to 1024
    D. 300 to 600

47. A language that is designed to specify the layout of a document is known as a(n) _____ 47.____
language.

    A. object-oriented
    B. query
    C. assembly
    D. markup

48. A hacker enters the computer system of his credit card company and changes a charge 48.____
from $1,250.00 to $12.50. This is an example of the computer crime known as

    A. Van Eck bugging
    B. salami attack
    C. piggybacking
    D. data diddling

49. In the hexadecimal coding system, 1111 equals the 49.____

    A. number two
    B. number four
    C. letter D
    D. letter F

50. A URL may include information about 50.____
    I. what protocol to use
    II. the IP address
    III. the domain name
    IV. the type of file

    A. I and II
    B. II and III
    C. II, III and IV
    D. I, II, III and IV

KEY (CORRECT ANSWERS)

1. C	11. C	21. D	31. D	41. D
2. B	12. A	22. B	32. C	42. D
3. B	13. D	23. A	33. C	43. B
4. C	14. B	24. C	34. A	44. A
5. A	15. B	25. A	35. B	45. A
6. A	16. D	26. D	36. D	46. B
7. A	17. C	27. A	37. A	47. D
8. B	18. C	28. A	38. A	48. D
9. A	19. C	29. C	39. B	49. D
10. C	20. C	30. D	40. D	50. D

TEST 2

DIRECTIONS: Each question or incomplete statement is followed by several suggested answers or completions. Select the one the BEST answers the question or completes the statement. *PRINT THE LETTER OF THE CORRECT ANSWER IN THE SPACE AT THE RIGHT.*

1. Because of their vertical arrangement, the OSI Reference Model and the TCP/IP protocols are referred to as network protocol   1.____

    A. towers
    B. stacks
    C. dunes
    D. compilers

2. _____ of the operating system are less frequently used, and copied from the disk as needed.   2.____

    A. Nonresident
    B. Peripheral
    C. Application
    D. Unthreaded

3. Presentation programs such as PowerPoint often use the _____ effect to blend slides together while switching from one to the next.   3.____

    A. dithering
    B. transition
    C. slumping
    D. fade-in

4. In a network in which transactions are being recorded, the _____ strategy is designed to ensure that either all the databases on the network are updated or none of them, so that the databases remain synchronized.   4.____

    A. dynaset
    B. two-phase commit
    C. failover
    D. aggregate function

5. Which of the following is an optical storage device?   5.____

    A. CD-ROM
    B. Floppy disk
    C. Hard disk
    D. Cassette tape

6. The capacity of RAM is measured in   6.____

    A. bytes
    B. kilobytes
    C. megabytes
    D. gigabytes

7. The four stages of the CPU's operation cycle, in sequence, are   7.____

    A. execute, store, decode, fetch
    B. fetch, execute, translate, store
    C. fetch, decode, execute, store
    D. encode, store, decode, fetch

8. In a database application, a _____ check validation would ensure that a worker's salary   8.____
did not exceed the maximum of $53,599.

    A. range
    B. completeness
    C. sequence
    D. consistency

9. In a _____ network, all nodes have equivalent capabilities and responsibilities.   9.____

    A. peer-to-peer
    B. file server
    C. frame relay
    D. client/server

10. Which of the following is NOT a common technology for the storage of binary informa-   10.____
tion?

    A. Analog
    B. Magnetic
    C. Optical
    D. Electronic

11. Typically, the term "legacy application" is applied to   11.____

    A. productivity software
    B. newer, more innovative programs
    C. database management systems
    D. operating systems

12. Which of the following is NOT an example of a database application?   12.____

    A. Parts inventory system
    B. Automated teller machine
    C. Mortgage calculator
    D. Flight reservations system

13. A computer component may signal the CPU that it has data available by   13.____

    A. shorting the bus
    B. fetching an instruction
    C. flushing the pipeline
    D. sending an interrupt

14. The hexadecimal numbering system uses a base of   14._____

    A. eight
    B. twelve
    C. sixteen
    D. thirty-two

15. POSIX is   15._____

    A. a set of standards to make applications independent of the UNIX operating system
    B. an open-source alternative to the UNIX operating system
    C. a set of standards that makes an operating system look like UNIX to an application
    D. a specialized form of the UNIX operating system for use in medical/ health care applications

16. The type of programming language that most closely mirrors human ways of thinking is   16._____
_____ language.

    A. assembly
    B. object-oriented
    C. translator
    D. query

17. The main reason hard disks are used to store data instead of much faster technologies,   17._____
such as DRAM, is because hard disks are

    A. capable of reorganizing data from location to location
    B. less prone to read/write errors
    C. more amenable to recovery if something goes wrong
    D. not volatile

18. The final step in producing an executable program is to   18._____

    A. translate pseudocode into source code
    B. translate the source code into object code
    C. translate source code into a language such as C or FORTRAN
    D. transform the object code into machine language

19. What is the term for software that has been written into ROM?   19._____

    A. Warez
    B. Pseudocode
    C. Firmware
    D. Macrocode

20. Variables play an important role in computer programming because they enable pro-   20._____
grammers to

    A. maintain strict quality-control standards
    B. make programs backward compatible
    C. avoid repeated iterations
    D. write flexible programs

21. The foremost organization for information systems personnel and managers is the   21.____

    A. Data Processing Management Association
    B. United States Chief Information Officers Council
    C. Information Resources Management Association
    D. Association of Internet Professionals

22. Second-generation graphics systems improved upon first-generation systems by   22.____

    A. adding shading capabilities
    B. supporting texture-mapping
    C. allowing for the movement of objects in 3D space
    D. enabling full-scene antialiasing

23. Suitable standards for testing the quality of a computer program include each of the following, EXCEPT   23.____

    A. semantic errors
    B. logic errors
    C. robustness
    D. reliability

24. Bitmap file formats include each of the following, EXCEPT   24.____

    A. GIF
    B. CGM
    C. PNG
    D. DIB

25. The largest collection of information in a database is the   25.____

    A. file
    B. system
    C. field
    D. record

26. Of the telephone technologies listed below, the oldest is   26.____

    A. FDDI
    B. PSTN
    C. SONET
    D. ISDN

27. The primary difference between a "workstation" and a regular desktop system lies in   27.____

    A. graphics capabilities
    B. the operating system
    C. microprocessing speeds
    D. the number of users

28. In contemporary personal computers, the stripped-down operating system is stored in _____ before a computer is turned on.

    28.____

    A. RAM
    B. ROM
    C. the hard disk
    D. the CPU

29. When a computer is multitasking, the _____ controls the flow of program tasks through the CPU.

    29.____

    A. RAM
    B. CPU
    C. disk cache
    D. operating system

30. A digital pulse, viewed on an oscilloscope, appears as a

    30.____

    A. square wave
    B. short dash
    C. microwave
    D. gamma wave

31. The first operating system developed with preemptive multitasking was

    31.____

    A. MS-DOS
    B. OS/2
    C. Windows
    D. UNIX

32. Each of the following methods of data compression may involve temporal compression, EXCEPT

    32.____

    A. JPEG
    B. Content-based
    C. MPEG
    D. P-frame

33. A network manager is considering the implementation of ATM technology. Because the organization uses the network primarily for file transfers, the most appropriate type of ATM service would be _____ bit rate.

    33.____

    A. available
    B. variable
    C. constant
    D. unspecified

34. Which type of color model is typically used in commercial printing?

    34.____

    A. CIE
    B. RGB
    C. HGB
    D. CMYK

35. The _____ is an allotted space in which spreadsheet programs allow users to create   35._____
and edit data and formulas.

    A. register
    B. formula bar
    C. data field
    D. status bar

36. The four-layered protocol that was instrumental in the expansion of the Internet is   36._____

    A. OSI
    B. ATM
    C. TCP/IP
    D. UDP/IP

37. The most common top-level domain name suffix used on the World Wide Web is   37._____

    A. .gov
    B. .edu
    C. .org
    D. .com

38. The process of synchronizing databases that exist in different localities is known as   38.

    A. replication
    B. distribution
    C. storehousing
    D. backup

39. Productivity software that uses a document-centric approach is made possible by the   39._____
compound document standards known as

    A. XML and HTML
    B. VAP and AWT
    C. JFS and ISAM
    D. OLE and OpenDoc

40. What is the term for a WAN or LAN that uses TCP/IP protocols and can be accessed   40._____
only by users from within the organization that owns the network?

    A. Extranet
    B. Intranet
    C. Supranet
    D. Isonet

41. File compression technologies that attempt to eliminate redundant or unnecessary infor-   41._____
mation, such as the technology used with MPEG files, are described as

    A. terse
    B. DCT
    C. lossy
    D. stripped

42. What is the term for a database that is designed to help managers make strategic business decisions?   42._____

    A. Data mine
    B. Operational data store
    C. Data mart
    D. Data warehouse

43. Which type of computer virus exploits the automatic command execution capabilities of certain types of application software?   43._____

    A. Macro virus
    B. Worm
    C. Trojan horse
    D. Zombie

44. All computers use a _____ to translate between digital code and audio signals.   44._____

    A. sound card
    B. SMDI
    C. audio scrubber
    D. Sound Blaster

45. A hard disk's storage capacity can be increased by means of   45._____

    A. caching
    B. virtual memory
    C. boot blocking
    D. file compression

46. _____ a standard for describing the location of resources on the World Wide Web.   46._____

    A. FTP
    B. URL
    C. XML
    D. HTML

47. Which of the following is a multithreading operating system?   47._____

    A. UNIX
    B. MS-DOS
    C. VMS
    D. Linux

48. Probably the easiest method for committing computer crime today is   48._____

    A. shoulder surfing
    B. piggybacking
    C. Trojan horses
    D. below-threshold attacks

49. Which of the following types of servers enables users to log on to a host computer and perform tasks as if they're working on the remote computer itself?   49.____

    A. Middleware
    B. Telnet
    C. IRC
    D. FTP

50. _____ occurs when a programmer places source code and a compiler or interpreter on a different computer platform, and then creates working object code.   50.____

    A. Assembling
    B. Reconfiguring
    C. Replication
    D. Porting

KEY (CORRECT ANSWERS)

1. B	11. C	21. A	31. D	41. C
2. A	12. C	22. A	32. A	42. C
3. B	13. D	23. A	33. D	43. A
4. B	14. C	24. B	34. D	44. A
5. A	15. C	25. A	35. B	45. D
6. A	16. B	26. B	36. C	46. B
7. C	17. D	27. A	37. D	47. D
8. A	18. D	28. B	38. A	48. A
9. A	19. C	29. D	39. D	49. B
10. A	20. D	30. A	40. B	50. D

EXAMINATION SECTION
TEST 1

DIRECTIONS: Each question or incomplete statement is followed by several suggested answers or completions. Select the one the BEST answers the question or completes the statement. *PRINT THE LETTER OF THE CORRECT ANSWER IN THE SPACE AT THE RIGHT.*

1. Object-oriented programming languages include each of the following, EXCEPT   1._____

    A. Java
    B. Ada
    C. Smalltalk
    D. C++

2. _____ is a programming language that is good for processing numerical data, but does   2._____
not lend itself very well to organizing large programs.

    A. Pascal
    B. Java
    C. FORTRAN
    D. COBOL

3. Which of the following is a method for insuring that a transmitted message has not been   3._____
tampered with?

    A. Indexing
    B. Hashing
    C. Stringing
    D. Spoofing

4. Many expert systems use _____ programming, which is characterized by programs that   4._____
are self-learning.

    A. algorithmic
    B. natural-language
    C. heuristic
    D. neural

5. Data transfer rates for devices such as hard disks are typically measured in   5._____

    A. Kbps
    B. KBps
    C. Mbps
    D. MBps

6. The most powerful way of requesting information from a database is through the use of   6._____
a(n)

    A. query language
    B. menu parameter(s)
    C. query by example (QBE)
    D. query string

7. A network of computers located within a limited geographic area usually, a single building or group of buildingsis known as a(n)

    A. Server farm
    B. LAN
    C. MAN
    D. token ring

    7.____

8. Viewing video presentations on the Web sometimes requires the use of an additional software program that adds functionality to a browser. This program is called a(n)

    A. plug-in
    B. grain
    C. applet
    D. script

    8.____

9. In a _____ attack, a criminal exploits limits in the TCP/IP protocol to flood a network with useless traffic and bring it to a standstill.

    A. spoofing
    B. denial-of-service
    C. wire closet
    D. logic bomb

    9.____

10. What is the term used for the technique used by some Web sites to deliver one page to a search engine for indexing while serving an entirely different page to everyone else?

    A. Diddling
    B. Port scanning
    C. Spamming
    D. Cloaking

    10.____

11. _____ is a method for checking data transmission errors in which bits are added to the message and then compared against a bit that says whether the sum should be odd or even.

    A. Cyclic redundancy checking
    B. Parity checking
    C. Checksum
    D. MNP

    11.____

12. A storage device's most important performance attribute is measured as

    A. latency
    B. access time
    C. permanence
    D. density

    12.____

13. Most contemporary personal computers contain a CPU with a register that is _____ bits wide.

    A. 8   B. 16   C. 32   D. 64

    13.____

14. A Web user wants to use a search engine for a particular color or pattern. What type of   14.____
    search should be used?

    A. Image content
    B. Raster-pixel
    C. Keyword
    D. Picot

15. An important difference between a router and a switcher is that a router   15.____

    A. does not perform error correction
    B. operates in software
    C. often suffers from interference
    D. is selective about the type of data it handles

16. Which of the following terms differs from the others in meaning?   16.____

    A. Software interrupt
    B. Exception
    C. Burst
    D. Trap

17. Which of the following is a database, used by the Windows operating system, that con-   17.____
    tains information about installed peripherals and software?

    A. Configuration
    B. Registry
    C. Finder
    D. Directory

18. A network server typically uses its own _____ to manage the flow of network data.   18.____

    A. RAM cache
    B. database management system
    C. virtual memory
    D. operating system

19. Which of the following types of firewall techniques applies security mechanisms when-   19.____
    ever a TCP or UDP connection is made?

    A. Packet filter
    B. Proxy server
    C. Application gateway
    D. Circuit-level gateway

20. The frequent creation, deletion, and modification of files on a computer hard drive often   20.____
    leads to the condition known as

    A. clustering
    B. optimization
    C. partitioning
    D. fragmentation

21. Engineers or architects often use an output device known as a _____ to create large   21.____
    drawings.

    A. banner
    B. LED printer
    C. plotter
    D. thermal printer

22. In most application software, utilities such as the spell checker are usually included in the   22.____
    _____ menu.

    A. file
    B. edit
    C. help
    D. tools

23. The primary factor driving the use of telephone networks for the provision of Internet ser-   23.____
    vices throughout its first two decades was

    A. collusion between ISPs and telephone companies
    B. a lack of more suitable technologies
    C. the widespread availability of hardware and protocols
    D. the existence of analog coding for data

24. CPU clock speeds are expressed in   24.____

    A. nanoseconds
    B. MHz
    C. seconds
    D. Mbps

25. If a filename includes an extension, a(n) _____ separates the extension from the rest of   25.____
    the filename.

    A. period
    B. backslash
    C. parentheses
    D. space

26. Database software that uncovers previously unknown relationships among data—for   26.____
    example, that would reveal customers with common interests—is described as _____
    software.

    A. drilldown
    B. warehousing
    C. on-line analytical processing (OLAP)
    D. data mining

27. Which of the following is a technology that combines the guaranteed delivery of circuit-   27.____
    switched networks and the robustness and efficiency of packet-switching networks?

    A. Frame relay
    B. DWDM
    C. SONET
    D. ATM

28. Advantages of vector graphics over bitmapped graphics include   28.____
    I.   easier manipulation of images
    II. smaller memory requirements
    III. greater scalability
    IV. more refined output

    A. I and II
    B. II only
    C. II and III
    D. I, II, III and IV

29. Which of the following types of translator programs works on one line of source code at a   29.____
    time before execution?

    A. modulator
    B. assembler
    C. compiler
    D. interpreter

30. The protocol developed by Netscape for transmitting private documents over the Internet   30.____
    is

    A. Secure HTTP
    B. IPsec
    C. Secure Sockets Layer (SSL)
    D. Layer 2 Tunneling Protocol (L2TP)

31. _____ specifies the format of URLs and the procedure clients and servers follow to   31.____
    communicate.

    A. TCP/IP
    B. FTP
    C. HTTP
    D. HTML

32. In the 1990s, significant advancements were made in each of the following portable com-   32.____
    puting technologies, EXCEPT

    A. graphics
    B. battery performance
    C. networking capabilities
    D. storage capacity

33. Each of the following is a multimedia input device, EXCEPT   33.____

    A. image scanner
    B. digital camera
    C. microphone
    D. video camcorder

34. In a_____ network, there is no file server.   34._____

    A. two-tier
    B. three-tier
    C. peer-to-peer
    D. thin client

35. When an operating system runs different parts of a program on different processors, it is   35._____
performing

    A. multiprocessing
    B. multitasking
    C. multithreading
    D. task switching

36. Hard disks   36._____
    I.   generally allow for a high density of bits
    II.   are much faster than floppy disks
    III. can improve their performance through caching
    IV.   are the most economical form of storage

    A. I and II
    B. I, II and III
    C. II, III and IV
    D. I, II, III and IV

37. To represent a single color on a computer screen, at least _____ color values must be   37._____
used.

    A. 2
    B. 3
    C. 4
    D. 5

38. The increasing popularity of the Linux operating system has been due to the fact that it is   38._____
    I.   available for free
    II.   platform-independent
    III. more secure than other operating systems
    IV.   more user-friendly than other operating systems

    A. I and II
    B. I, II and III
    C. II only
    D. I, II, III and IV

39. The total package of protocols that specifies how a specific network functions is known   39._____
as the protocol

    A. suite
    B. train
    C. stack
    D. milieu

40. Another term for the autonumber field in a database management system is _____ field.   40.____

    A. calculated
    B. key
    C. counter
    D. computational

41. Operating systems can be used to   41.____
    I.   communicate with a printer
    II. format disks
    III. control the mouse cursor
    IV. save files

    A. I and II
    B. II and III
    C. II, III and IV
    D. I, II, III and IV

42. XML is a development in networking technology whose most significant contribution is in the area of   42.____

    A. functionality
    B. scalability
    C. economy
    D. interoperability

43. The most significant difference between computer viruses and Trojan horses is that   43.____

    A. Trojan horses are not destructive
    B. Trojan horses do not replicate themselves
    C. most firewalls are not built to withstand Trojan horses
    D. viruses are not disguised as useful programs

44. Slide presentation applications such as PowerPoint allow users to resize a frame within a slide by means of dragging   44.____

    A. text
    B. borders
    C. handles
    D. flaps

45. Each of the following serve to translate object code into machine language, EXCEPT   45.____

    A. binders
    B. linkers
    C. assemblers
    D. compilers

46. The most important difference between the Macintosh operating system and MS-DOS is the   46.____

    A. memory requirements
    B. functionality of drivers
    C. interface
    D. multitasking capabilities

47. Which of the following is a looser, more basic way of organizing data in order to support   47.____
    management decision-making?

    A. Data mart
    B. Data mine
    C. Data vault
    D. Data warehouse

48. What is the term for the amount of data that can be transmitted over a network during a   48.____
    fixed period of time?

    A. Bandwidth
    B. Frequency
    C. Packet volume
    D. Amplitude

49. The OSI (Open System Interconnection) model defines a networking framework for   49.____
    implementing protocols in seven layers. The first layer of the OSI model consists of

    A. the network
    B. transport
    C. applications
    D. hardware/physical components

50. Many paint and draw programs organize complex drawings by means of tools known as   50.____

    A. vectors
    B. sectors
    C. layers
    D. models

———

KEY (CORRECT ANSWERS)

1.	B	11.	B	21.	C	31.	C	41.	D
2.	C	12.	B	22.	D	32.	B	42.	D
3.	B	13.	C	23.	C	33.	A	43.	B
4.	C	14.	A	24.	B	34.	C	44.	C
5.	D	15.	B	25.	A	35.	A	45.	D
6.	A	16.	C	26.	D	36.	B	46.	C
7.	B	17.	B	27.	D	37.	B	47.	D
8.	A	18.	D	28.	C	38.	A	48.	A
9.	B	19.	D	29.	D	39.	A	49.	D
10.	D	20.	D	30.	C	40.	C	50.	C

TEST 2

DIRECTIONS: Each question or incomplete statement is followed by several suggested answers or completions. Select the one the BEST answers the question or completes the statement. *PRINT THE LETTER OF THE CORRECT ANSWER IN THE SPACE AT THE RIGHT.*

1. The "physical layer" of a network would include each of the following, EXCEPT   1.____

    A. RAM
    B. Error correction
    C. Virtual memory
    D. Data organization on disk

2. Servers   2.____

    A. are not designed to be used directly by the user
    B. function solely to manage network traffic
    C. often perform tasks other than their server tasks
    D. are not "computers" in the strictest sense of the word

3. Advantages of using RISC CPUs in personal computers include   3.____
       I. fewer transistors required
      II. rapid execution of instructions
      III. smaller burden placed on software

    A. I only
    B. I and II
    C. II and III
    D. I, II and III

4. Which of the following is NOT an example of middleware?   4.____

    A. Object request broker (ORB)
    B. Web server
    C. TP monitor
    D. Database access system

5. The main disadvantage to the bus network topology is its   5.____

    A. centralized point of failure
    B. high data error frequency
    C. tendency to bottleneck
    D. extensive cabling

6. Java, C++, and Perl are examples of   6.____

    A. query languages
    B. program languages
    C. markup languages
    D. application programs

7. The most significant obstacle organizations face when they try to implement ERP soft-   7._____
   ware is

   A. training personnel
   B. data migration
   C. reshaping business practices to conform to the system
   D. managing the up-front hardware investment

8. A storage disk's concentric circles of information, or tracks, are divided into subsections   8._____
   known as

   A. arcs   B. blocks   C. sectors   D. radii

9. In the client-server architecture, an ORB is sometimes necessary to   9._____

   A. provide error-checking between client and server
   B. translate the languages and protocols of distributed elements
   C. patrol the firewalls surrounding network servers
   D. help the client locate a file on a particular server

10. An office worker is proofreading a speech transcribed by a colleague. The previous   10._____
    worker has repeatedly and consistently misspelled the word "fiscal" as "physical." In a
    word processing application, the tool for automatically changing each of the misspellings
    is the

    A. undo command
    B. find and replace
    C. cut and paste
    D. spelling and grammar checker

11. The programs that enable a computer and its peripheral devices to function smoothly are   11._____
    known collectively as the

    A. operating system
    B. BIOS
    C. system software
    D. driver set

12. The act of registering a popular Internet addressusually a company name-with the intent   12._____
    of selling it to its rightful owner is known as

    A. spoofing
    B. steganography
    C. warchalking
    D. cybersquatting

13. A relational database management system (RDBMS) is BEST described as a database   13._____
    that

    A. groups related fields together in a single table
    B. organized around groups of records that have a common field value
    C. stores data in a set of associated tables
    D. helps to analyze large clusters of records

14. In object-oriented programming, a class of objects sometimes uses portions of another   14.____
    class in order to extend its functionality. This is a process known as

    A. inheritance
    B. annexation
    C. overlay
    D. torque

15. In digital communications, the assurance that a transferred message has been sent and   15.____
    received by the parties claiming to have sent and received the message is known as

    A. nonrepudiation
    B. private key encryption
    C. packet sniffing
    D. certification

16. In the hexadecimal coding system, the sequence 01001000 would represent   16.____

    A. ABC
    B. 2AC
    C. 48
    D. 136

17. The most important impact of legacy applications on software developers is a(n)   17.____

    A. large amount of time spent rewriting old code
    B. complication of bundled sales
    C. necessity for sticking with an older programming language
    D. limit placed on the functionality of new software

18. Copyrighted software that is delivered/downloaded free of charge, but requires a regis-   18.____
    tration free for those who decide to keep it and use it, is known as

    A. abandonware
    B. freeware
    C. public-domain software
    D. shareware

19. _____ is a programming language that embodies powerful object-oriented features, but   19.____
    is complex and difficult to learn.

    A. C++
    B. Java
    C. Pascal
    D. COBOL

20. A router detects network congestion in each of the following ways, EXCEPT   20.____

    A. average queue lengths
    B. choke packet totals
    C. percentage of buffers in use
    D. line utilization

21. A Web site or service that offers a broad array of resources and services, such as e-mail, forums, search engines, and on-line shopping mallsis often referred to as a(n)　21.____

    A. site map
    B. browser
    C. host
    D. portal

22. In most Web page design software,　22.____
    I.　a WYSIWYG interface is used
    II.　the user is required to answer all given questions before results can be viewed
    III.　the software produces HTML code
    IV.　hotspots are created

    A. I and III
    B. I, III and IV
    C. II, III and IV
    D. I, II, III and IV

23. The primary difference between XML and HTML is that XML　23.____

    A. is tied to a particular applications and hardware types
    B. specifies what each data tag means
    C. contains built-in security features
    D. uses tags only to delimit items of data, and leaves interpretation up to the application that created a file

24. In draw programs, each line in a drawing is defined as a　24.____

    A. voxel
    B. bitmap
    C. pixel
    D. vector

25. "Distributions" of the Linux operating system include each of the following, EXCEPT　25.____

    A. Corel
    B. Solaris
    C. Red Hat
    D. Debian

26. Depending on the operating system, filenames may　26.____
    I.　include extensions that indicate the type of file
    II.　be limited in length
    III.　not be permitted to use certain characters
    IV.　make use of "wildcard" characters for selecting multiple files with a single selection

    A. I only
    B. I, II and III
    C. II and III
    D. I, II, III and IV

27. The "fax revolution" came about by the gradual blending of telecommunications, optical scanning, and printing technologies into a single device. This is an example of the phenomenon known as

    A. synergy
    B. coincidence
    C. asymmetry
    D. convergence

27.____

28. The security protocol most widely deployed over virtual private networks is

    A. IPsec
    B. Layer 2 tunneling protocol (L2TP)
    C. Point-to-point tunneling protocol (PPTP)
    D. Secure sockets layer (SSL)

28.____

29. The SVGA display standard supports a resolution of

    A. 640 x 480
    B. 720 x 400
    C. 800 x 600
    D. 1024 x 768

29.____

30. The expansion problems of the bus network topology are most easily solved by introducing a hub and forming a _____ topology.

    A. star
    B. line
    C. ring
    D. tree

30.____

31. When an operating system runs different parts of a program on the same processor at different times, it is performing

    A. multithreading
    B. time-sharing
    C. task switching
    D. multiprocessing

31.____

32. For long distance links, the most suitable wireless technology is

    A. radio frequencies
    B. infrared
    C. microwaves
    D. optics

32.____

33. In packet-switching networks, packets contain each of the following, EXCEPT their

    A. route through the network
    B. address of origin
    C. destination address
    D. data

33.____

34. The unit of information that precedes a data object in packet transmission, and which contains transparent information about the file or transmission, is the   34.____

   A. payload   B. comptroller   C. hash   D. header

35. What is the general term for a message given to a Web browser by a Web server?   35.____

   A. Trojan horse
   B. Cookie
   C. Token
   D. Spyware

36. In the URL *http://www.technophobia.com/index.html,* the domain name is   36.____

   A. .com
   B. technophobia.com
   C. http://www.technophobia.com
   D. technophobia

37. The purpose of a driver is to   37.____

   A. keep the CPU running at a minimum clock speed
   B. keep the bus free of interference
   C. enable the operating system to communicate with a device
   D. manage memory

38. Data on the Internet can often be manipulated dishonestly to further the agenda of the people using the data. Such methods of data manipulation include   38.____
     I. standard deviation
     II. false relevance
     III. skewed sample
     IV. deduction

   A. I and II
   B. II and III
   C. II, III and IV
   D. I, II, III and IV

39. Any circuit board in a computer that is attached directly to another board is known as a(n)   39.____

   A. controller board
   B. expansion board
   C. adapter
   D. daughtercard

40. Which of the following types of viruses propagates by means of an infected program and installs itself on the first sector of the hard disk?   40.____

   A. Trojan horse
   B. Worm
   C. MBR virus
   D. Macro virus

41. Currently, the greatest advances in the field of artificial intelligence have occurred in the field of   41.____

    A. games playing
    B. neural networks
    C. robotics
    D. expert systems

42. Most laser printers require about _____ MB of RAM to print a full-page graphic at 300 dpi.   42.____

    A. 1
    B. 2
    C. 3
    D. 5

43. In a database application, a _____ check validation would ensure that a worker's benefit eligibility status was entered into a field, rather than his/her salary or other information.   43.____

    A. consistency
    B. format
    C. range
    D. sequence

44. Heuristic programs   44.____

    A. are based on mathematically provable procedures
    B. don't usually improve over time
    C. don't always reach the very best result, but usually produce a good result
    D. are most widely used in scientific modeling

45. Which of the following types of computer programs are most susceptible to virus attacks?   45.____

    A. Operating systems
    B. Database applications
    C. Compilers
    D. Web design applications

46. The main problem with having a "fragmented" hard disk is that   46.____

    A. retrieving data can be much slower
    B. the magnetic charge on the disk is weakened
    C. the disk cache is inhibited by interference
    D. it becomes impossible to move data from one location to another

47. The OSI (Open System Interconnection) model defines a networking framework for implementing protocols in seven layers. The _____ layer, or layer 5, establishes, manages and terminates connections between applications.   47.____

    A. Transport
    B. Data link
    C. Session
    D. Network

48. Management information systems are typically written in

    A. FORTRAN
    B. C
    C. COBOL
    D. BASIC

    48.____

49. Because each command is executed independently, without any knowledge of the commands that came before it, HTTP is described as a(n) _____ protocol.

    A. shallow
    B. isolate
    C. stateless
    D. marooned

    49.____

50. Advantages of fiber optic communications over traditional metal lines include
    I. greater bandwidth
    II. more lightweight
    III. less interference
    IV. sturdier and more durable

    A. I only
    B. I, II, III
    C. II and III
    D. I, II, III and IV

    50.____

———————

KEY (CORRECT ANSWERS)

1.	C	11.	C	21.	D	31.	B	41.	A
2.	A	12.	D	22.	B	32.	C	42.	A
3.	B	13.	C	23.	D	33.	A	43.	B
4.	B	14.	A	24.	D	34.	D	44.	C
5.	A	15.	A	25.	B	35.	B	45.	A
6.	B	16.	C	26.	D	36.	B	46.	A
7.	C	17.	D	27.	D	37.	C	47.	C
8.	C	18.	D	28.	A	38.	B	48.	C
9.	B	19.	A	29.	C	39.	D	49.	C
10.	B	20.	B	30.	A	40.	C	50.	B

EXAMINATION SECTION

TEST 1

DIRECTIONS: Each question or incomplete statement is followed by several suggested answers or completions. Select the one that BEST answers the question or completes the statement. *PRINT THE LETTER OF THE CORRECT ANSWER IN THE SPACE AT THE RIGHT.*

1. The primary storage is   1.____
   A. used by processor   B. used by RAM
   C. both A and B   D. none of the above

2. Clock speed is measured in   2.____
   A. hertz   B. megahertz
   C. gigahertz   D. none of the above

3. Which of the following temperatures can cause component failure?   3.____
   A. 180 degrees   B. 185 degrees   C. 190 degrees   D. 205 degrees

4. A motherboard has _____ connections to the power supply.   4.____
   A. one or more   B. just one
   C. two   D. none of the above

5. CMOS setup is used   5.____
   A. to change motherboard settings   B. for basic input/output
   C. both A and B   D. none of the above

6. ROM chips that can be overwritten are known as   6.____
   A. flash ROM   B. micro ROM
   C. BIOS   D. none of the above

7. A secure way of transferring files from one device to another is   7.____
   A. FTP   B. TFTP
   C. SFTP   D. none of the above

8. A method to provide access to a VPN is   8.____
   A. RAS   B. PPP   C. PPTP   D. IGP

9. A big advantage of having a wireless standard is   9.____
   A. interoperability between devices   B. greater device security
   C. both A and B   D. none of the above

10. When you are implementing a basic wireless network,   10.____
    A. disable ESSID broadcast   B. don't configure the ESSID point
    C. both A and B   D. none of the above

11. You are installing a device that can throttle and detect peer-to-peer traffic. This device belongs to the device type 11.____
    A. load balancer   B. bandwidth shaper
    C. proxy server   D. none of the above

12. The first step involved in troubleshooting after arriving on the site is 12.____
    A. identifying the symptoms and drawing a network diagram
    B. comparing wiring schematics to the industry standards
    C. both A and B
    D. none of the above

13. _____ describes an email that has web links to direct users to malicious websites. 13.____
    A. Phishing   B. Viruses
    C. Both A and B   D. None of the above

14. You are troubleshooting network connectivity and want to see the path that the packets are taking from a workstation to the server. The _____ command line tool will be used for this. 14.____
    A. ping   B. traceroute   C. route   D. nslookup

15. The process or steps required to be applied to develop an information system is 15.____
    A. system development life cycle   B. program specification
    C. design cycle   D. analytical code

16. Project plan is a document 16.____
    A. describing how the project team will develop the proposed system
    B. that outlines the technical feasibility of the proposed system
    C. both A and B
    D. none of the above

17. The primary goal of a system analyst is to 17.____
    A. create value for the organization   B. create a wonderful system
    C. acquire a working tool   D. none of the above

18. Understanding the purpose of the information system to be built and finding out how the project team is to accomplish making it is part of the _____ phase of the SDLC. 18.____
    A. analysis   B. system request
    C. planning   D. none of the above

19. Examining the economic, technical and organizational advantages and disadvantages of developing a new system is known as 19.____
    A. feasibility analysis   B. committee approval
    C. risk analysis   D. system request

20. The calculation measuring the amount of money an organization is going to get in return for the money it has spent is known as
    A. cash flow
    B. return on investment
    C. tangible costs
    D. none of the above

    20.____

21. New users should be encouraged to use software by taking help first from
    A. tutorial software
    B. training software
    C. both A and B
    D. none of the above

    21.____

22. A wizard is
    A. a person who can do magic
    B. software that helps and walks user through a complex process
    C. hardware that speeds up performance
    D. all of the above

    22.____

23. How can you determine the level of a trainee's knowledge?
    A. By watching them type
    B. By taking a test
    C. By asking them questions
    D. Both B and C

    23.____

24. Which of the following is the most important step when giving training users?
    A. Make them want to learn
    B. Push them until they master the task
    C. Leave learning or not learning up to them; just provide the training
    D. None of the above

    24.____

25. It is important that while training, the trainees are shown the
    A. training agenda
    B. results of previous training sessions
    C. trainer's achievements
    D. none of the above

    25.____

KEY (CORRECT ANSWERS)

1.	C		11.	B
2.	A		12.	A
3.	B		13.	A
4.	A		14.	B
5.	A		15.	A
6.	A		16.	A
7.	C		17.	A
8.	C		18.	C
9.	A		19.	A
10.	A		20.	B

21.	C
22.	B
23.	C
24.	A
25.	A

TEST 2

DIRECTIONS: Each question or incomplete statement is followed by several suggested answers or completions. Select the one that BEST answers the question or completes the statement. *PRINT THE LETTER OF THE CORRECT ANSWER IN THE SPACE AT THE RIGHT.*

1.   _____ makes it possible for the system to power up with the help of a   1._____
     keyboard.
     A. ACPI   B. APM
     C. Both A and B   D. None of the above

2.   Which of the following are data path sizes?   2._____
     A. 8, 16   B. 32, 64   C. 128   D. All of the above

3.   The lines that carry the data in a bus is known as   3._____
     A. data bus   B. memory bus
     C. micro bus   D. none of the above

4.   Which of the following can be used to boot, recover or reinstall the Windows   4._____
     operating system?
     A. Recovery CD   B. Windows CD
     C. Memory CD   D. None of the above

5.   Which of the following explains the proper handling of substances like   5._____
     chemical solvents?
     A. Material safety data sheet   B. POST
     C. Memory data sheet   D. None of the above

6.   A _____ tests a USB, networks, serial or other port.   6._____
     A. loop back plug   B. three-head plug
     C. both A and B   D. none of the above

7.   Bundling network cables can cause   7._____
     A. crosstalk   B. attenuation
     C. collision   D. none of the above

8.   The greatest concern while using an orbital satellite WAN link is   8._____
     A. cable length   B. duplex   C. latency   D. collision

9.   If packets to an IP address are dropping over the Internet, _____ will be   9._____
     used to determine the responsible hop.
     A. netstat   B. traceroute
     C. ping   D. none of the above

10. _____ ports can be used for FTP traffic.   10._____
     A. 25   B. 24   C. 23   D. 20

11. The _____ connects multiple workstations, functions as a router and supports VLANs.   11.____
    A. hub   B. multilayer switch
    C. switch   D. repeater

12. To provide VoIP phones with power but without having to arrange independent power supplies for them, the switches on the network should have   12.____
    A. spanning tree   B. PoE
    C. PPPoE   D. VLAN tagging

13. _____ has the same functionality as Telnet but operates more securely.   13.____
    A. SSH   B. RSH   C. TFTP   D. SNAT

14. You use a logical network diagram to determine the number of   14.____
    A. cables in the network
    B. broadcast domains on the network
    C. users on the network
    D. none of the above

15. Planning and controlling the system development within a deadline at the lowest cost and with the right functionality is called   15.____
    A. project management   B. task identification
    C. task   D. none of the above

16. One way of calculating project completion time is to apply industry standard factors for each phase of the project. In this method, the planning phase takes almost 15% of the total time. If a project takes three months for planning, then the remaining project will need approximately   16.____
    A. 20 months   B. 15 months
    C. 3 months   D. none of the above

17. Fourteen factors impact the complexity of a project when we are using a function point estimation worksheet. _____ are included in these factors.   17.____
    A. Data communications, end user efficiency and reusability
    B. Data communications, estimated effort and time tradeoffs
    C. Both A and B
    D. None of the above

18. In determining the tasks for a work plan, you can   18.____
    A. list the four phases of SDLC and steps occurring in each phase
    B. control and direct the project
    C. establish a possible reporting structure
    D. none of the above

19. If someone is examining existing paperwork so that he can better understand the As-Is system, this is   19.____
    A. observation   B. JAD
    C. document analysis   D. none of the above

20. _____ is an information-gathering technique that helps an analyst to find out facts and opinions from a large number of geographically dispersed people.
    A. Questionnaire   B. Document analysis
    C. JAD session   D. None of the above
    20.____

21. All of the following are examples of privacy and security risks EXCEPT
    A. viruses   B. spam
    C. hackers   D. Trojan horses
    21.____

22. _____ can recover a deleted/damaged file of a computer.
    A. Robotics   B. Simulation
    C. Both A and B   D. None of the above
    22.____

23. _____ language is used by the computer to process data.
    A. Binary   B. Processing
    C. Both A and B   D. None of the above
    23.____

24. The operating system
    A. enables drawing of a flowchart   B. provides user-friendly interface
    C. both A and B   D. none of the above
    24.____

25. _____ is not an application software package.
    A. Microsoft Office   B. Redhat Linux
    C. Adobe PageMaker   D. Microsoft PowerPoint
    25.____

KEY (CORRECT ANSWERS)

1.	A		11.	B
2.	D		12.	B
3.	A		13.	A
4.	A		14.	B
5.	A		15.	A
6.	A		16.	A
7.	A		17.	A
8.	C		18.	A
9.	B		19.	C
10.	D		20.	A

21.	B
22.	D
23.	A
24.	B
25.	B

TEST 3

DIRECTIONS: Each question or incomplete statement is followed by several suggested answers or completions. Select the one that BEST answers the question or completes the statement. *PRINT THE LETTER OF THE CORRECT ANSWER IN THE SPACE AT THE RIGHT.*

1. The character repeat rate can be adjusted in
    A. Control Panel > Keyboard   B. My Computer
    C. Recycle Bin   D. none of the above   1._____

2. There are _____ means of using a wireless mouse.
    A. 1   B. 2
    C. 3   D. none of the above   2._____

3. _____ is used for creating and manipulating sound.
    A. MIDI   B. SIDI
    C. MODO   D. None of the above   3._____

4. Picture quality is expressed in
    A. megapixels   B. hexapixels
    C. both of the above   D. none of the above   4._____

5. The microphone port is located on the
    A. sound card   B. motherboard
    C. driver   D. none of the above   5._____

6. The _____ is the peripheral device that transfers the audio from the PC.
    A. headphones   B. microphone
    C. camera   D. all of the above   6._____

7. _____ is a secure connection.
    A. HTTP   B. TELNET   C. HTTPs   D. RCP   7._____

8. A computer can be a client and a server to other computers in a _____
    network.
    A. bus   B. VPN   C. ring   D. peer-to-peer   8._____

9. A _____ is used to send a signal at one end of a cable and found at the other
    end of the cable.
    A. cable tester   B. toner probe
    C. multimeter   D. none of the above   9._____

10. A company's ISP uses _____ to troubleshoot network issues.
    A. Smart Jack   B. 110 Block   C. 66 Block   D. Demarc   10._____

11. A firewall has not blocked a remote web server. To verify this, a _____ can be
    used.   11._____
    A. port scanner   B. toner probe
    C. both A and B   D. none of the above

12. _____ should be enabled to prevent broadcast storms.   12._____
    A. Bonding   B. Spanning tree
    C. Port mirroring   D. DHCP

13. A _____ network is least likely to collide.   13._____
    A. bus   B. star   C. ring   D. mesh

14. _____ tests the operation of NIC.   14._____
    A. Crossover   B. Rollover   C. 568B   D. Loopback

15. Planning includes   15._____
    A. conducting preliminary investigation
    B. conducting feasibility study
    C. identifying constraints
    D. all of the above

16. Feasibility study types include   16._____
    A. technical   B. economic return
    C. non-economic return   D. all of the above

17. Analysis includes   17._____
    A. gathering competent team members
    B. sending instructions to users
    C. documenting the existing system
    D. all of the above

18. The design phase includes determining   18._____
    A. technical systems configuration   B. data structure
    C. make or buy decision   D. all of the above

19. Which one of the following is a type of documentation?   19._____
    A. System documentation   B. Document feeder
    C. Audio coding   D. None of the above

20. The implementation phase includes   20._____
    A. conducting cutover   B. training users
    C. managing change   D. all of the above

21. Processing takes place at the   21._____
    A. box   B. CPU   C. system unit   D. motherboard

22. Memory is of _____ type(s).   22._____
    A. one   B. two   C. three   D. four

23. The _____ card is used while playing a video game.   23.____
   A. sound   B. graphic
   C. modem   D. network information

24. To do a specific task, a set of instructions is given to the computer. This   24.____
most closely describes
   A. software   B. hardware
   C. Internet browsing   D. none of the above

25. A user is allowed to analyze and maintain a computer by a program called   25.____
   A. Utility   B. Windows XP
   C. MS Office   D. Device Driver

KEY (CORRECT ANSWERS)

1.	A		11.	A
2.	B		12.	B
3.	A		13.	C
4.	A		14.	D
5.	A		15.	D
6.	A		16.	D
7.	C		17.	C
8.	D		18.	D
9.	A		19.	A
10.	A		20.	D

21.	C
22.	B
23.	A
24.	A
25.	A

TEST 4

DIRECTIONS: Each question or incomplete statement is followed by several suggested answers or completions. Select the one that BEST answers the question or completes the statement. *PRINT THE LETTER OF THE CORRECT ANSWER IN THE SPACE AT THE RIGHT.*

1. A(n) _____ is a device resembling a hypodermic needle.
   A. extractor
   B. detracter
   C. loop back plug
   D. none of the above

   1._____

2. Which of the following are components of the microcomputer?
   A. Memory, Unit System
   B. Input device
   C. Output device
   D. All of the above

   2._____

3. _____ is a common type of keyboard.
   A. USB
   B. PS/2
   C. Both A and B
   D. None of the above

   3._____

4. How can we differentiate between a mouse's and keyboard's port?
   A. Keyboard is purple and mouse is green
   B. Keyboard is green and mouse is purple
   C. Keyboard is blue and mouse is green
   D. None of the above

   4._____

5. If you reboot your computer and receive an error message of BIOS keyboard,
   A. the mouse is plugged into the keyboard input
   B. the keyboard is plugged into the mouse input
   C. both A and B
   D. none of the above

   5._____

6. The mouse settings can be adjusted in
   A. Control Panel
   B. DOS
   C. My Computer
   D. none of the above

   6._____

7. _____ prevents the propagating of different departments network broadcasts if they are located on the same switch.
   A. Hub   B. VLAN   C. Firewall   D. Trunk

   7._____

8. The most secure protocol for transferring network device configuration is
   A. TFTP
   B. RCP
   C. SCP
   D. none of the above

   8._____

9. _____ Internet devices operate the OSI layer.
   A. One   B. Two   C. Three   D. Four

   9._____

10. You need to determine which buildings have multimode or single mode fiber. You will use the

    A. security policy   B. physical network diagram
    C. baseline configuration   D. none of the above

10.____

11. Many users are complaining about network issues. Of the following steps, which will you take FIRST?

    A. Collect information about the symptoms
    B. Make a plan of action and a solution
    C. Document the solution
    D. None of the above

11.____

12. Employees utilizing wireless laptops outdoors at the office are experiencing new connectivity problems. _____ is/are most likely causing the problems.

    A. Signal bounce   B. Antenna distance
    C. Environment factors   D. None of the above

12.____

13. The _____ contain(s) information about unlabeled data center connections.

    A. wiring schematics   B. emergency call list
    C. procedures manual   D. none of the above

13.____

14. If you have to install a phone that needs only one wire for both data and power to be supplied, _____ must be supported by the switch.

    A. PoE   B. spanning tree
    C. VLAN   D. none of the above

14.____

15. During the analysis phase, _____ is the type of prototype.

    A. discovery   B. evolving
    C. functioning   D. none of the above

15.____

16. _____ is a review technique that checks the validity of the documents produced during system analysis.

    A. Structured walkthrough   B. Prototyping
    C. Joint application   D. None of the above

16.____

17. Implementation classes

    A. describe the user interface   B. show implementation rules
    C. describe database interactions   D. none of the above

17.____

18. Databases and file definition are prepared in the _____ phase.

    A. implementation   B. design
    C. analysis   D. none of the above

18.____

19. _____ is requirements analysis deliverables.

    A. Requirement specification   B. User manual
    C. Design specification   D. All of the above

19.____

20. _____ can help an analyst to work with users to find out system usage.   20.____
    A. Use case   B. Class
    C. Actor   D. None of the above

21. _____ is a data-transfer technique.   21.____
    A. DMA   B. CAD
    C. Both A and B   D. None of the above

22. _____ devices are designed under electromechanical principle.   22.____
    A. Input   B. Output
    C. Storage   D. All of the above

23. A monitor consists of   23.____
    A. BRT   B. ARU
    C. CRT   D. none of the above

24. Exception is also known as   24.____
    A. interrupt   B. traps
    C. system calls   D. none of the above

25. _____ is a mutually exclusive operation.   25.____
    A. Signal instruction   B. Wait instruction
    C. Both A and B   D. None of the above

_____

KEY (CORRECT ANSWERS)

1.	A	11.	A
2.	D	12.	C
3.	C	13.	A
4.	A	14.	A
5.	C	15.	A
6.	A	16.	A
7.	B	17.	A
8.	C	18.	A
9.	C	19.	A
10.	B	20.	A

21.	A
22.	A
23.	C
24.	C
25.	C

_____

EXAMINATION SECTION
TEST 1

DIRECTIONS: Each question or incomplete statement is followed by several suggested answers or completions. Select the one that BEST answers the question or completes the statement. *PRINT THE LETTER OF THE CORRECT ANSWER IN THE SPACE AT THE RIGHT.*

1. When deciding the means by which training is to be delivered, the designer of instruction should FIRST select the

    A. type of delivery system technology
    B. trainer
    C. necessary instructional properties
    D. delivery system

1.____

2. _____ does NOT directly involve instruction, but offers the power to make learning more efficient.

    A. Computer-managed instruction (CMI)
    B. Computer-based training (CBT)
    C. Technical training function (TTF)
    D. Computer-assisted instruction (CAI)

2.____

3. The use of case studies as a means of instructional delivery should be avoided when

    A. training involves management or supervisory personnel
    B. instructional goals include critical thinking
    C. there is unhealthy competition among trainees
    D. time constraints on preparation exist

3.____

4. Each of the following is a function of audience response systems (ARS) software EXCEPT

    A. analyzing group responses to items
    B. performing demographic analyses
    C. storing scores for later analysis
    D. administering progressive evaluations during instruction

4.____

5. Which of the following is a step typically involved in the design phase of instructional design?

    A. Pilot instruction
    B. Developing instructional materials
    C. Analyzing job tasks
    D. Developing testing strategies

5.____

6. Which of the following is NOT a typical component of a performance support system (PSS)?

    A. Expert system   B. Printed job aids
    C. Text retrieval   D. Computer-aided instruction

6.____

7. An expert system includes knowledge structured for capturing regularly occurring cir-   7._____
cumstances. This structured knowledge is known as

   A. logic
   B. frames
   C. neural network processing
   D. rules

8. In a training situation, a(n) _____ is MOST likely to be held liable for misrepresentation.   8._____

   A. employer
   B. outside contractors/vendors
   C. owner/employer
   D. trainer

9. A good computer-assisted instruction delivery system will use   9._____

   A. norming   B. scrolling
   C. page-turning   D. branching

10. Each of the following is usually considered to be a characteristic of effective instructional   10._____
design EXCEPT

   A. rule-based design   B. holistic self-evaluation
   C. interconnected tasks   D. systematic approach

11. Instructional media are typically used to   11._____

   A. direct learning activities
   B. predict the best method of instructional delivery
   C. support learning activities
   D. evaluate trainee performance

12. Which of the following instructional delivery techniques typically involves the LOWEST   12._____
development cost?

   A. Audiotape   B. Multimedia computer
   C. Lecture   D. Live video

13. Computer-aided instruction is often designed so that only the precise knowledge needed   13._____
at that point in the activity is taught.
This is referred to as _____ CAI.

   A. secular   B. granular
   C. partitioned   D. modular

14. Each of the following is an advantage associated with the use of vendors as trainers   14._____
EXCEPT

   A. no additional strain on training budget
   B. initiation of function that can later be turned over to in-house trainer
   C. usual offering of continued support
   D. proficiency in using new equipment or machines

15. Which of the following is a mode of computer-supported learning resources?　　15._____

    A. Evaluation　　　　　　　　　B. Tutorial
    C. Instructional games　　　　　D. Hypermedia

16. Which of the following conditions does NOT typically indicate the use of performance　16._____
support devices?

    A. Regulation requirements
    B. Frequently changing tasks
    C. Infrequently performed tasks
    D. Cost of mistakes is relatively low

17. Which of the following performance support devices can MOST accurately be described　17._____
as *procedural?*

    A. Printed job aids
    B. Computer-based references (CBR)
    C. Hypertext
    D. Computer help systems

18. If a typical instructor-led training delivery system requires ten hours of instructional time,　18._____
a textual computer-based training approach will typically require about _____ instructional hours.

    A. 40　　　　B. 100　　　　C. 200　　　　D. 400

19. Which of the following is an advantage associated with the use of performance observa-　19._____
tion as a means of gathering data during instructional design?

    A. Immediate response availability
    B. Minimal disturbance in work routines
    C. Generation of motivational information
    D. Low relative cost

20. Each of the following is a mode of computer-managed instruction EXCEPT　　20._____

    A. record keeping　　　　　B. simulation
    C. prescription generation　　D. testing

21. Which of the following is typically addressed in the evaluation strategy produced during　21._____
instructional design?

    A. Balance of activities encompassed by the design
    B. Development of instructional materials
    C. Outcomes required to satisfy each performance criterion
    D. Provision of learner reinforcement

22. As a means of instructional delivery, role playing is useful under each of the following　22._____
conditions EXCEPT when

    A. training involves the application of content knowledge
    B. technical or psychomotor skills are the focus
    C. training involves management or supervisory personnel
    D. instructional objectives are concerned with interpersonal relations

23. _____ is NOT a step typically involved in the analysis phase of instructional design.   23.____

    A. Writing instructional objectives
    B. Selecting tasks for training
    C. Determining instructional prerequisites
    D. Assessing learning requirements

24. Instruction delivered to new employees before they begin regular work is called_____   24.____
training.

    A. OJT   B. vestibule
    C. independent study   D. apprenticeship

25. If a company decides to contract out to an external training provider, each of the following   25.____
elements must be included in a request for proposal EXCEPT

    A. project background   B. outputs and deliverables
    C. delivery strategy   D. project procedures

KEY (CORRECT ANSWERS)

1. C		11. C	
2. A		12. C	
3. D		13. B	
4. D		14. B	
5. D		15. D	
6. B		16. D	
7. B		17. A	
8. B		18. C	
9. D		19. B	
10. B		20. B	

21. C
22. B
23. C
24. B
25. C

TEST 2

DIRECTIONS: Each question or incomplete statement is followed by several suggested answers or completions. Select the one that BEST answers the question or completes the statement. *PRINT THE LETTER OF THE CORRECT ANSWER IN THE SPACE AT THE RIGHT.*

1. It is a good idea to use lecturing as a method of instructional delivery when   1.____

   A. complex processes need to be explained
   B. introducing training provided by other methods or media
   C. the trainer is unfamiliar with the audience
   D. instructional goals deal with affective or psycho-motor skills

2. Typically, the LARGEST part of all training costs is   2.____

   A. job aids
   B. vendor contracts
   C. travel expense associated with off-site training
   D. trainee salary during training

3. The systemic approach to training evaluation is typically divided into four parts. Which of the following is NOT one of these parts?   3.____

   A. Identification of trainee prerequisites
   B. Identification of training goals
   C. Production of learning outcomes
   D. Support performance development

4. During the instructional design process, an analysis document is produced which includes specifications for each of the following EXCEPT   4.____

   A. measurement factors
   B. target audience characteristics
   C. instructional media
   D. program management

5. Each of the following is a disadvantage associated with the use of employee-trainers EXCEPT   5.____

   A. least economical for recurrent training needs
   B. increased head count in labor budget
   C. less likely to have knowledge of adult learning techniques
   D. lack of knowledge of new-hire trainers

6. Which of the following is NOT among the modes of computer-assisted instruction?   6.____

   A. Problem solving   B. Calculation
   C. Modeling   D. Drill and practice

7. Which of the following performance support devices offers the GREATEST availability to trainees?   7.____

   A. Printed job aids   B. Expert systems
   C. Hypertext   D. Computer help systems

8. Demonstrations might be used as a method of instructional delivery when

    A. instructional goals involve cognitive or affective domains
    B. dealing with especially large groups of trainees
    C. tasks require manual dexterity or are difficult for learners to understand
    D. when materials and equipment are scarce

8.____

9. Which of the following is typically addressed during the implementation phase of instructional design?

    A. Revision of instructional materials
    B. Selection of tasks for training
    C. Creation of design syllabus
    D. Creation of delivery strategy

9.____

10. The psychomotor domain of learning progresses in four discrete stages. Which of the following stages is typically the LAST to be accomplished?

    A. Manipulation   B. Articulation
    C. Imitation   D. Precision

10.____

11. A well-written instructional objective should include three key components. Which of the following is NOT one of these?

    A. Conditions   B. Performance
    C. Media   D. Criteria

11.____

12. If a job requires high technical knowledge but low manual skill, which of the following learning methods would be BEST suited for job training?

    A. Self-study and lab
    B. Classroom and on-the-job training with mentor
    C. Classroom and lab
    D. Classroom and self-practice

12.____

13. The computer- _____ component of technology-based training does NOT actually teach or manage instruction, but serves to make learning easier and more appropriate.

    A. managed instruction (CMI)
    B. based training (CBT)
    C. supported learning resource (CSLR)
    D. assisted instruction (CAI)

13.____

14. _____ simulation is used in information systems training.

    A. Manual   B. Hybrid
    C. Sequential   D. Computer

14.____

15. In order for trainees to move nonsequentially through a computerized training document, _____ will need to be installed.

    A. an expert system   B. hypertext
    C. an authoring system   D. a hierarchy

15.____

16. If a job requires high technical knowledge and manual skill, which of the following learning methods would be BEST suited for job training?

    A. Self-study and lab
    B. Classroom and on-the-job training with mentor
    C. Classroom and lab
    D. Classroom and self-practice

16.____

17. Which of the following is typically addressed in the design syllabus created during instructional design?

    A. Sequence in which content is presented
    B. Evaluation of training objectives
    C. Means of administering precourse assessment
    D. Evaluation of prerequisite skills

17.____

18. The use of peer tutoring as a method of instructional delivery will usually have all of the following benefits EXCEPT

    A. facilitating pacing of instruction in groups with heterogeneous abilities
    B. encouraging competition among trainees
    C. easing trainer"s workload
    D. increasing trainee's satisfaction with instruction

18.____

19. Which of the following instructional delivery techniques typically offers the GREATEST opportunity for self-pacing?

    A. Audiotape   B. Multimedia computer
    C. Lecture   D. Live video

19.____

20. In the development of technology-based training, the logical starting point is computer-

    A. managed instruction (CMI)
    B. based training (CBT)
    C. supported learning resources (CSLR)
    D. assisted instruction (CAI)

20.____

21. As a means of instructional delivery, case studies are MOST useful for

    A. very large groups of trainees
    B. bridging theory and practice
    C. shaping attitudinal objectives
    D. drill and practice of psychomotor skills

21.____

22. An advantage commonly associated with the use of consultants as trainers is

    A. employees may be able to earn college credit for training course
    B. no increase in labor budget
    C. availability for modular training
    D. *one-shot* training

22.____

23. Discussion should be avoided as a method of instructional delivery when

    A. dealing with a group of trainees that is forty or larger
    B. content is rigid and restricted to facts
    C. there are strict time constraints on instruction
    D. instructional goals deal with attitudes or critical thinking skills

23.____

24. The component of technology-based learning that actually teaches is   24.____

   A. computer-managed instruction (CMI)
   B. computer-based training (CBT)
   C. technical training function (TTF)
   D. computer-assisted instruction (CAI)

25. Which of the following instructional delivery approaches would typically require the FEW-   25.____
   EST number of development hours?

   A. Textual computer-based training
   B. Workbook
   C. Videotape
   D. Instructor-led

_____

KEY (CORRECT ANSWERS)

1.	B		11.	C
2.	D		12.	D
3.	A		13.	C
4.	C		14.	D
5.	A		15.	B
6.	B		16.	B
7.	A		17.	A
8.	C		18.	B
9.	A		19.	B
10.	B		20.	A

21.	B
22.	B
23.	C
24.	D
25.	D

_____

GLOSSARY OF COMPUTER TERMS

Contents

GLOSSARY OF COMPUTER TERMS

Basic

application & app
An application (often called "app" for short) is simply a program with a GUI. Note that it is different from an applet.

boot
Starting up an OS is booting it. If the computer is already running, it is more often called rebooting.

browser
A browser is a program used to browse the web. Some common browsers include Netscape, MSIE (Microsoft Internet Explorer), Safari, Lynx, Mosaic, Amaya, Arena, Chimera, Opera, Cyberdog, HotJava, etc.

bug
A bug is a mistake in the design of something, especially software. A really severe bug can cause something to crash.

chat
Chatting is like e-mail, only it is done instantaneously and can directly involve multiple people at once. While e-mail now relies on one more or less standard protocol, chatting still has a couple competing ones. Of particular note are IRC and Instant Messenger. One step beyond chatting is called MUDding.

click
To press a mouse button. When done twice in rapid succession, it is referred to as a double-click.

cursor
A point of attention on the computer screen, often marked with a flashing line or block. Text typed into the computer will usually appear at the cursor.

database
A database is a collection of data, typically organized to make common retrievals easy and efficient. Some common database programs include Oracle, Sybase, Postgres, Informix, Filemaker, Adabas, etc.

desktop
A desktop system is a computer designed to sit in one position on a desk somewhere and not move around. Most general purpose computers are desktop systems. Calling a system a desktop implies nothing about its platform. The fastest desktop system at any given time is typically either an Alpha or PowerPC based system, but the SPARC and PA-RISC based systems are also often in the running. Industrial strength desktops are typically called workstations.

directory
Also called "folder", a directory is a collection of files typically created for organizational purposes. Note that a directory is itself a file, so a directory can generally contain other directories. It differs in this way from a partition.

disk
A disk is a physical object used for storing data. It will not forget its data when it loses power. It is always used in conjunction with a disk drive. Some disks can be removed from their drives, some cannot. Generally it is possible to write new information to a disk in addition to reading data from it, but this is not always the case.

drive
A device for storing and/or retrieving data. Some drives (such as disk drives, zip drives, and tape drives) are typically capable of having new data written to them, but some others (like CD-ROMs or DVD-ROMs) are not. Some drives have random access (like disk drives, zip drives, CD-ROMs, and DVD-ROMs), while others only have sequential access (like tape drives).

e-book
The concept behind an e-book is that it should provide all the functionality of an ordinary book but in a manner that is (overall) less expensive and more environmentally friendly. The actual term e-book is somewhat confusingly used to refer to a variety of things: custom software to play e-book titles, dedicated hardware to play e-book titles, and the e-book titles themselves. Individual e-book titles can be free or commercial (but will always be less expensive than their printed counterparts) and have to be loaded into a player to be read. Players vary wildly in capability level. Basic ones allow simple reading and bookmarking; better ones include various features like hypertext, illustrations, audio, and even limited video. Other optional features allow the user to mark-up sections of text, leave notes, circle or diagram things, highlight passages, program or customize settings, and even use interactive fiction. There are many types of e-book; a couple popular ones include the Newton book and Palm DOC.

e-mail
E-mail is short for electronic mail. It allows for the transfer of information from one computer to another, provided that they are hooked up via some sort of network (often the Internet. E-mail works similarly to FAXing, but its contents typically get printed out on the other end only on demand, not immediately and automatically as with FAX. A machine receiving e-mail will also not reject other incoming mail messages as a busy FAX machine will; rather they will instead be queued up to be received after the current batch has been completed. E-mail is only seven-bit clean, meaning that you should not expect anything other than ASCII data to go through uncorrupted without prior conversion via something like uucode or bcode. Some mailers will do some conversion automatically, but unless you know your mailer is one of them, you may want to do the encoding manually.

file
A file is a unit of (usually named) information stored on a computer.

firmware
Sort of in-between hardware and software, firmware consists of modifiable programs embedded in hardware. Firmware updates should be treated with care since they can literally destroy the underlying hardare if done improperly. There are also cases where neglecting to apply a firmware update can destroy the underlying hardware, so user beware.

floppy
An extremely common type of removable disk. Floppies do not hold too much data, but most computers are capable of reading them. Note though that there are different competing format used for floppies, so that a floppy written by one type of computer might not directly work on another. Also sometimes called "diskette".

format
The manner in which data is stored; its organization. For example, VHS, SVHS, and Beta are three different formats of video tape. They are not 100% compatible with each other, but information can be transferred from one to the other with the proper equipment (but not always without loss; SVHS contains more information than either of the other two). Computer information can be stored in literally hundreds of different formats, and can represent text, sounds, graphics, animations, etc. Computer information can be exchanged via different computer types provided both computers can interpret the format used.

function keys
On a computer keyboard, the keys that start with an "F" that are usually (but not always) found on the top row. They are meant to perform user-defined tasks.

graphics
Anything visually displayed on a computer that is not text.

hardware
The physical portion of the computer.

hypertext
A hypertext document is like a text document with the ability to contain pointers to other regions of (possibly other) hypertext documents.

Internet
The Internet is the world-wide network of computers. There is only one Internet, and thus it is typically capitalized (although it is sometimes referred to as "the 'net"). It is different from an intranet.

keyboard
A keyboard on a computer is almost identical to a keyboard on a typewriter. Computer keyboards will typically have extra keys, however. Some of these keys (common examples include Control, Alt, and Meta) are meant to be used in conjunction with other keys just like shift on a regular typewriter. Other keys (common examples include Insert, Delete, Home, End, Help, function keys,etc.) are meant to be used independently and often perform editing tasks. Keyboards on different platforms will often look slightly different and have somewhat different collections of keys. Some keyboards even have independent shift lock and caps lock keys. Smaller keyboards with only math-related keys are typically called "keypads".

language
Computer programs can be written in a variety of different languages. Different languages are optimized for different tasks. Common languages include Java, C, C++, ForTran, Pascal, Lisp, and BASIC. Some people classify languages into two categories, higher-level and lower-level. These people would consider assembly language and machine language lower-level languages and all other languages higher-level. In general, higher-level languages can be either interpreted or compiled; many languages allow both, but some are restricted to one or the other. Many people do not consider machine language and assembly language at all when talking about programming languages.

laptop
A laptop is any computer designed to do pretty much anything a desktop system can do but run for a short time (usually two to five hours) on batteries. They are designed to be carried around but are not particularly convenient to carry around. They are significantly more expensive than desktop systems and have far worse battery life than PDAs. Calling a system a laptop implies nothing about its platform. By far the fastest laptops are the PowerPC based Macintoshes.

memory
Computer memory is used to temporarily store data. In reality, computer memory is only capable of remembering sequences of zeros and ones, but by utilizing the binary number system it is possible to produce arbitrary rational numbers and through clever formatting all manner of representations of pictures, sounds, and animations. The most common types of memory are RAM, ROM, and flash.

MHz & megahertz
One megahertz is equivalent to 1000 kilohertz, or 1,000,000 hertz. The clock speed of the main processor of many computers is measured in MHz, and is sometimes (quite misleadingly) used to represent the overall speed of a computer. In fact, a computer's speed is based upon many factors, and since MHz only reveals how many clock cycles the main processor has per second (saying nothing about how much is actually accomplished per cycle), it can really only accurately be used to gauge two computers with the same generation and family of processor plus similar configurations of memory, co-processors, and other peripheral hardware.

modem
A modem allows two computers to communicate over ordinary phone lines. It derives its name

from **mod**ulate / **dem**odulate, the process by which it converts digital computer data back and forth for use with an analog phone line.

monitor

The screen for viewing computer information is called a monitor.

mouse

In computer parlance a mouse can be both the physical object moved around to control a pointer on the screen, and the pointer itself. Unlike the animal, the proper plural of computer mouse is "mouses".

multimedia

This originally indicated a capability to work with and integrate various types of things including audio, still graphics, and especially video. Now it is more of a marketing term and has little real meaning. Historically the Amiga was the first multimedia machine. Today in addition to AmigaOS, IRIX and Solaris are popular choices for high-end multimedia work.

NC

The term **n**etwork **c**omputer refers to any (usually desktop) computer system that is designed to work as part of a network rather than as a stand-alone machine. This saves money on hardware, software, and maintenance by taking advantage of facilities already available on the network. The term "Internet appliance" is often used interchangeably with NC.

network

A network (as applied to computers) typically means a group of computers working together. It can also refer to the physical wire etc. connecting the computers.

notebook

A notebook is a small laptop with similar price, performance, and battery life.

organizer

An organizer is a tiny computer used primarily to store names, addresses, phone numbers, and date book information. They usually have some ability to exchange information with desktop systems. They boast even better battery life than PDAs but are far less capable. They are extremely inexpensive but are typically incapable of running any special purpose applications and are thus of limited use.

OS

The **o**perating **s**ystem is the program that manages a computer's resources. Common OSes include Windows '95, MacOS, Linux, Solaris, AmigaOS, AIX, Windows NT, etc.

PC

The term **p**ersonal **c**omputer properly refers to any desktop, laptop, or notebook computer system. Its use is inconsistent, though, and some use it to specifically refer to x86 based systems running MS-DOS, MS-Windows, GEOS, or OS/2. This latter use is similar to what is meant by a WinTel system.

PDA

A **p**ersonal **d**igital **a**ssistant is a small battery-powered computer intended to be carried around by the user rather than left on a desk. This means that the processor used ought to be power-efficient as well as fast, and the OS ought to be optimized for hand-held use. PDAs typically have an instant-on feature (they would be useless without it) and most are grayscale rather than color because of battery life issues. Most have a pen interface and come with a detachable stylus. None use mouses. All have some ability to exchange data with desktop systems. In terms of raw capabilities, a PDA is more capable than an organizer and less capable than a laptop (although some high-end PDAs beat out some low-end laptops). By far the most popular PDA is the Pilot, but other common types include Newtons, Psions, Zauri, Zoomers, and Windows CE hand-helds. By far the fastest current PDA is the Newton (based around a StrongARM RISC processor). Other PDAs are optimized for other tasks; few computers are as personal as PDAs and care must be taken in their purchase. Feneric's PDA / Handheld Comparison Page is perhaps the most detailed comparison of PDAs and handheld computers to be found anywhere on the web.

platform
Roughly speaking, a platform represents a computer's family. It is defined by both the processor type on the hardware side and the OS type on the software side. Computers belonging to different platforms cannot typically run each other's programs (unless the programs are written in a language like Java).

portable
If something is portable it can be easily moved from one type of computer to another. The verb "to port" indicates the moving itself.

printer
A printer is a piece of hardware that will print computer information onto paper.

processor
The processor (also called central processing unit, or CPU) is the part of the computer that actually works with the data and runs the programs. There are two main processor types in common usage today: CISC and RISC. Some computers have more than one processor and are thus called "multiprocessor". This is distinct from multitasking. Advertisers often use megahertz numbers as a means of showing a processor's speed. This is often extremely misleading; megahertz numbers are more or less meaningless when compared across different types of processors.

program
A program is a series of instructions for a computer, telling it what to do or how to behave. The terms "application" and "app" mean almost the same thing (albeit applications generally have GUIs). It is however different from an applet. Program is also the verb that means to create a program, and a programmer is one who programs.

run
Running a program is how it is made to do something. The term "execute" means the same thing.

software
The non-physical portion of the computer; the part that exists only as data; the programs. Another term meaning much the same is "code".

spreadsheet
An program used to perform various calculations. It is especially popular for financial applications. Some common spreadsheets include Lotus 123, Excel, OpenOffice Spreadsheet, Octave, Gnumeric, AppleWorks Spreadsheet, Oleo, and GeoCalc.

user
The operator of a computer.

word processor
A program designed to help with the production of textual documents, like letters and memos. Heavier duty work can be done with a desktop publisher. Some common word processors include MS-Word, OpenOffice Write, WordPerfect, AbiWord, AppleWorks Write, and GeoWrite.

www
The World-Wide-Web refers more or less to all the publically accessible documents on the Internet. It is used quite loosely, and sometimes indicates only HTML files and sometimes FTP and Gopher files, too. It is also sometimes just referred to as "the web".

Reference

65xx

The 65xx series of processors includes the 6502, 65C02, 6510, 8502, 65C816, 65C816S, etc. It is a CISC design and is not being used in too many new stand-alone computer systems, but is still being used in embedded systems, game systems (such as the Super NES), and processor enhancement add-ons for older systems. It was originally designed by MOS Technologies, but is now produced by The Western Design Center, Inc. It was the primary processor for many extremely popular systems no longer being produced, including the Commodore 64, the Commodore 128, and all the Apple][series machines.

68xx

The 68xx series of processors includes the 6800, 6805, 6809, 68000, 68020, 68030, 68040, 68060, etc. It is a CISC design and is not being used in too many new stand-alone computer systems, but is still being used heavily in embedded systems. It was originally designed by Motorola and was the primary processor for older generations of many current machines, including Macintoshes, Amigas, Sun workstations, HP workstations, etc. and the primary processor for many systems no longer being produced, such as the TRS-80. The PowerPC was designed in part to be its replacement.

a11y

Commonly used to abbreviate the word "accessibility". There are eleven letters between the "a" and the "y".

ADA

An object-oriented language at one point popular for military and some academic software. Lately C++ and Java have been getting more attention.

AI

Artificial intelligence is the concept of making computers do tasks once considered to require thinking. AI makes computers play chess, recognize handwriting and speech, helps suggest prescriptions to doctors for patients based on imput symptoms, and many other tasks, both mundane and not.

AIX

The industrial strength OS designed by IBM to run on PowerPC and x86 based machines. It is a variant of UNIX and is meant to provide more power than OS/2.

AJaX

AJaX is a little like DHTML, but it adds asynchronous communication between the browser and Web site via either XML or JSON to achieve performance that often rivals desktop applications.

Alpha

An Alpha is a RISC processor invented by Digital and currently produced by Digital/Compaq and Samsung. A few different OSes run on Alpha based machines including Digital UNIX, Windows NT, Linux, NetBSD, and AmigaOS. Historically, at any given time, the fastest processor in the world has usually been either an Alpha or a PowerPC (with sometimes SPARCs and PA-RISCs making the list), but Compaq has recently announced that there will be no further development of this superb processor instead banking on the release of the somewhat suspect Merced.

AltiVec

AltiVec (also called the "Velocity Engine") is a special extension built into some PowerPC CPUs to provide better performance for certain operations, most notably graphics and sound. It is similar to MMX on the x86 CPUs. Like MMX, it requires special software for full performance benefits to be realized.

Amiga

A platform originally created and only produced by Commodore, but now owned by Gateway 2000 and produced by it and a few smaller companies. It was historically the first multimedia machine and gave the world of computing many innovations. It is now primarily used for audio / video applications; in fact, a decent Amiga system is less expensive than a less capable video editing system. Many music videos were created on Amigas, and a few television series and movies had their special effects generated on Amigas. Also, Amigas can be readily synchronized with video cameras, so typically when a computer screen appears on television or in a movie and it is not flickering wildly, it is probably an Amiga in disguise. Furthermore, many coin-operated arcade games are really Amigas packaged in stand-up boxes. Amigas have AmigaOS for their OS. New Amigas have either a PowerPC or an Alpha for their main processor and a 68xx processor dedicated to graphics manipulation. Older (and low end) Amigas do everything with just a 68xx processor.

AmigaOS

The OS used by Amigas. AmigaOS combines the functionality of an OS and a window manager and is fully multitasking. AmigaOS boasts a pretty good selection of games (many arcade games are in fact written on Amigas) but has limited driver support. AmigaOS will run on 68xx, Alpha, and PowerPC based machines.

Apple][

The Apple][computer sold millions of units and is generally considered to have been the first home computer with a 1977 release date. It is based on the 65xx family of processors. The earlier Apple I was only available as a build-it-yourself kit.

AppleScript

A scripting language for Mac OS computers.

applet

An applet differs from an application in that is not meant to be run stand-alone but rather with the assistance of another program, usually a browser.

AppleTalk

AppleTalk is a protocol for computer networks. It is arguably inferior to TCP/IP.

Aqua

The default window manager for Mac OS X.

Archie

Archie is a system for searching through FTP archives for particular files. It tends not to be used too much anymore as more general modern search engines are significantly more capable.

ARM

An ARM is a RISC processor invented by Advanced RISC Machines, currently owned by Intel, and currently produced by both the above and Digital/Compaq. ARMs are different from most other processors in that they were not designed to maximize speed but rather to maximize speed per power consumed. Thus ARMs find most of their use on hand-held machines and PDAs. A few different OSes run on ARM based machines including Newton OS, JavaOS, and (soon) Windows CE and Linux. The StrongARM is a more recent design of the original ARM, and it is both faster and more power efficient than the original.

ASCII

The ASCII character set is the most popular one in common use. People will often refer to a bare text file without complicated embedded format instructions as an ASCII file, and such files can usually be transferred from one computer system to another with relative ease. Unfortunately there are a few minor variations of it that pop up here and there, and if you receive a text file that seems subtly messed up with punctuation marks altered or upper and lower case reversed, you are probably encountering one of the ASCII variants. It is usually fairly straightforward to translate from one ASCII variant to another, though. The ASCII character set is seven bit while pure binary is usually eight bit, so transferring a binary file through ASCII channels will result in corruption and loss of data. Note also that the ASCII character set is a subset of the Unicode character set.

ASK

A protocol for an infrared communications port on a device. It predates the IrDA compliant infrared communications protocol and is not compatible with it. Many devices with infrared communications support both, but some only support one or the other.

assembly language

Assembly language is essentially machine language that has had some of the numbers replaced by somewhat easier to remember mnemonics in an attempt to make it more human-readable. The program that converts assembly language to machine language is called an assembler. While assembly language predates FORTRAN, it is not typically what people think of when they discuss computer languages.

Atom

Atom is an intended replacement for RSS and like it is used for syndicating a web site's content. It is currently not nearly as popular or well-supported by software applications, however.

authoring system

Any GUIs method of designing new software can be called an authoring system. Any computer language name with the word "visual" in front of it is probably a version of that language built with some authoring system capabilities. It appears that the first serious effort to produce a commercial quality authoring system took place in the mid eighties for the Amiga.

AWK

AWK is an interpreted language developed in 1977 by Aho, Weinberger, & Kernighan. It gets its name from its creators' initials. It is not particularly fast, but it was designed for creating small throwaway programs rather than full-blown applications -- it is designed to make the writing of the program fast, not the program itself. It is quite portable with versions existing for numerous platforms, including a free GNU version. Plus, virtually every version of UNIX in the world comes with AWK built-in.

BASIC

The Beginners' All-purpose Symbolic Instruction Code is a computer language developed by Kemeny & Kurtz in 1964. Although it is traditionally interpreted, compilers exist for many platforms. While the interpreted form is typically fairly slow, the compiled form is often quite fast, usually faster than Pascal. The biggest problem with BASIC is portability; versions for different machines are often completely unlike each other; Amiga BASIC at first glance looks more like Pascal, for example. Portability problems actually go beyond even the cross platform level; in fact, most machines have multiple versions of incompatible BASICs available for use. The most popular version of BASIC today is called Visual BASIC. Like all BASICs it has portability issues, but it has some of the advantages of an authoring system so it is relatively easy to use.

baud

A measure of communications speed, used typically for modems indicating how many bits per second can be transmitted.

BBS

A bulletin board system is a computer that can be directly connected to via modem and provides various services like e-mail, chatting, newsgroups, and file downloading. BBSs have waned in popularity as more and more people are instead connecting to the Internet, but they are still used for product support and local area access. Most current BBSs provide some sort of gateway connection to the Internet.

bcode

Identical in intent to uucode, bcode is slightly more efficient and more portable across different computer types. It is the preferred method used by MIME.

BeOS

A lightweight OS available for both PowerPC and x86 based machines. It is often referred to simply as "Be".

beta

A beta version of something is not yet ready for prime time but still possibly useful to related developers and other interested parties. Expect beta software to crash more than properly released software does. Traditionally beta versions (of commercial software) are distributed only to selected testers who are often then given a discount on the proper version after its release in exchange for their testing work. Beta versions of non-commercial software are more often freely available to anyone who has an interest.

binary

There are two meanings for binary in common computer usage. The first is the name of the number system in which there are only zeros and ones. This is important to computers because all computer data is ultimately a series of zeros and ones, and thus can be represented by binary numbers. The second is an offshoot of the first; data that is not meant to be intepreted through a common character set (like ASCII) is typically referred to as binary data. Pure binary data is typically eight bit data, and transferring a binary file through ASCII channels without prior modification will result in corruption and loss of data. Binary data can be turned into ASCII data via uucoding or bcoding.

bit

A bit can either be on or off; one or zero. All computer data can ultimately be reduced to a series of bits. The term is also used as a (very rough) measure of sound quality, color quality, and even procesor capability by considering the fact that series of bits can represent binary numbers. For example (without getting too technical), an eight bit image can contain at most 256 distinct colors while a sixteen bit image can contain at most 65,536 distinct colors.

bitmap

A bitmap is a simplistic representation of an image on a computer, simply indicating whether or not pixels are on or off, and sometimes indicating their color. Often fonts are represented as bitmaps. The term "pixmap" is sometimes used similarly; typically when a distinction is made, pixmap refers to color images and bitmap refers to monochrome images.

blog

Short for web log, a blog (or weblog, or less commonly, 'blog) is a web site containing periodic (usually frequent) posts. Blogs are usually syndicated via either some type of RSS or Atom and often supports TrackBacks. It is not uncommon for blogs to function much like newspaper columns. A blogger is someone who writes for and maintains a blog.

boolean

Boolean algebra is the mathematics of base two numbers. Since base two numbers have only two values, zero and one, there is a good analogy between base two numbers and the logical values "true" & "false". In common usage, booleans are therefore considered to be simple logical values like true & false and the operations that relate them, most typically "and", "or" and "not". Since everyone has a basic understanding of the concepts of true & false and basic conjunctions, everyone also has a basic understanding of boolean concepts -- they just may not realize it.

byte

A byte is a grouping of bits. It is typically eight bits, but there are those who use non-standard byte sizes. Bytes are usually measured in large groups, and the term "kilobyte" (often abbreviated as K) means one-thousand twenty-four (1024) bytes; the term "megabyte" (often abbreviated as M) means one-thousand twenty-four (1024) K; the term gigabyte (often abbreviated as G) means one-thousand twenty-four (1024) M; and the term "terabyte" (often abbreviated as T) means one-thousand twenty-four (1024) G. Memory is typically measured in kilobytes or megabytes, and disk space is typically measured in megabytes or gigabytes. Note that the multipliers here are 1024 instead of the more common 1000 as would be used in the metric system. This is to make it easier to work with the binary number system. Note also that some hardware manufacturers will use the smaller 1000 multiplier on M & G quantities to make

10

their disk drives seem larger than they really are; buyer beware.

bytecode

Sometimes computer languages that are said to be either interpreted or compiled are in fact neither and are more accurately said to be somewhere in between. Such languages are compiled into bytecode which is then interpreted on the target system. Bytecode tends to be binary but will work on any machine with the appropriate runtime environment (or virtual machine) for it.

C

C is one of the most popular computer languages in the world, and quite possibly *the* most popular. It is a compiled langauge widely supported on many platforms. It tends to be more portable than FORTRAN but less portable than Java; it has been standardized by ANSI as "ANSI C" -- older versions are called either "K&R C" or "Kernighan and Ritchie C" (in honor of C's creators), or sometimes just "classic C". Fast and simple, it can be applied to all manner of general purpose tasks. C compilers are made by several companies, but the free GNU version (gcc) is still considered one of the best. Newer C-like object-oriented languages include both Java and C++.

C#

C# is a compiled object-oriented language based heavily on C++ with some Java features.

C++

C++ is a compiled object-oriented language. Based heavily on C, C++ is nearly as fast and can often be thought of as being just C with added features. It is currently probably the second most popular object-oriented language, but it has the drawback of being fairly complex -- the much simpler but somewhat slower Java is probably the most popular object-oriented language. Note that C++ was developed independently of the somewhat similar Objective-C; it is however related to Objective-C++.

C64/128

The Commodore 64 computer to this day holds the record for being the most successful model of computer ever made with even the lowest estimates being in the tens of millions. Its big brother, the Commodore 128, was not quite as popular but still sold several million units. Both units sported ROM-based BASIC and used it as a default "OS". The C128 also came with CP/M (it was a not-often-exercized option on the C64). In their later days they were also packaged with GEOS. Both are based on 65xx family processors. They are still in use today and boast a friendly and surprisingly active user community. There is even a current effort to port Linux to the C64 and C128 machines.

CDE

The common desktop environment is a popular commercial window manager (and much more -- as its name touts, it is more of a desktop environment) that runs under X-Windows. Free work-alike versions are also available.

chain

Some computer devices support chaining, the ability to string multiple devices in a sequence plugged into just one computer port. Often, but not always, such a chain will require some sort of terminator to mark the end. For an example, a SCSI scanner may be plugged into a SCSI CD-ROM drive that is plugged into a SCSI hard drive that is in turn plugged into the main computer. For all these components to work properly, the scanner would also have to have a proper terminator in use. Device chaining has been around a long time, and it is interesting to note that C64/128 serial devices supported it from the very beginning. Today the most common low-cost chainable devices in use support USB while the fastest low-cost chainable devices in use support FireWire.

character set

Since in reality all a computer can store are series of zeros and ones, representing common things like text takes a little work. The solution is to view the series of zeros and ones instead as

156

a sequence of bytes, and map each one to a particular letter, number, or symbol. The full mapping is called a character set. The most popular character set is commonly referred to as ASCII. The second most popular character set these days is Unicode (and it will probably eventually surpass ASCII). Other fairly common character sets include EBCDIC and PETSCII. They are generally quite different from one another; programs exist to convert between them on most platforms, though. Usually EBCDIC is only found on really old machines.

CISC

Complex instruction set computing is one of the two main types of processor design in use today. It is slowly losing popularity to RISC designs; currently all the fastest processors in the world are RISC. The most popular current CISC processor is the x86, but there are also still some 68xx, 65xx, and Z80s in use.

CLI

A command-line interface is a text-based means of communicating with a program, especially an OS. This is the sort of interface used by MS-DOS, or a UNIX shell window.

COBOL

The **Co**mmon **B**usiness **O**riented **L**anguage is a language developed back in 1959 and still used by some businesses. While it is relatively portable, it is still disliked by many professional programmers simply because COBOL programs tend to be physically longer than equivalent programs written in almost any other language in common use.

compiled

If a program is compiled, its original human-readable source has been converted into a form more easily used by a computer prior to it being run. Such programs will generally run more quickly than interpreted programs, because time was pre-spent in the compilation phase. A program that compiles other programs is called a compiler.

compression

It is often possible to remove redundant information or capitalize on patterns in data to make a file smaller. Usually when a file has been compressed, it cannot be used until it is uncompressed. Image files are common exceptions, though, as many popular image file formats have compression built-in.

cookie

A cookie is a small file that a web page on another machine writes to your personal machine's disk to store various bits of information. Many people strongly detest cookies and the whole idea of them, and most browsers allow the reception of cookies to be disabled or at least selectively disabled, but it should be noted that both Netscape and MSIE have silent cookie reception enabled by default. Sites that maintain shopping carts or remember a reader's last position have legitimate uses for cookies. Sites without such functionality that still spew cookies with distant (or worse, non-existent) expiration dates should perhaps be treated with a little caution.

CP/M

An early DOS for desktops, CP/M runs on both Z80 and the x86 based machines. CP/M provides only a CLI and there really is not any standard way to get a window manager to run on top of it. It is fairly complex and tricky to use. In spite of all this, CP/M was once the most popular DOS and is still in use today.

crash

If a bug in a program is severe enough, it can cause that program to crash, or to become inoperable without being restarted. On machines that are not multitasking, the entire machine will crash and have to be rebooted. On machines that are only partially multitasking the entire machine will sometimes crash and have to be rebooted. On machines that are fully multitasking, the machine should never crash and require a reboot.

Cray

A Cray is a high-end computer used for research and frequently heavy-duty graphics applications. Modern Crays typically have Solaris for their OS and sport sixty-four RISC

processors; older ones had various other configurations. Current top-of-the-line Crays can have over 2000 processors.

crippleware

Crippleware is a variant of shareware that will either self-destruct after its trial period or has built-in limitations to its functionality that get removed after its purchase.

CSS

Cascading style sheets are used in conjunction with HTML and XHTML to define the layout of web pages. While CSS is how current web pages declare how they should be displayed, it tends not to be supported well (if at all) by ancient browsers. XSL performs this same function more generally.

desktop publisher

A program for creating newspapers, magazines, books, etc. Some common desktop publishing programs include FrameMaker, PageMaker, InDesign, and GeoPublish.

DHTML

Dynamic HTML is simply the combined use of both CSS and JavaScript together in the same document; a more extreme form is called AJaX. Note that DHTML is quite different from the similarly named DTML.

dict

A protocol used for looking up definitions across a network (in particular the Internet).

digital camera

A digital camera looks and behaves like a regular camera, except instead of using film, it stores the image it sees in memory as a file for later transfer to a computer. Many digital cameras offer additional storage besides their own internal memory; a few sport some sort of disk but the majority utilize some sort of flash card. Digital cameras currently lack the resolution and color palette of real cameras, but are usually much more convenient for computer applications. Another related device is called a scanner.

DIMM

A physical component used to add RAM to a computer. Similar to, but incompatible with, SIMMs.

DNS

Domain name service is the means by which a name (like www.saugus.net or ftp.saugus.net) gets converted into a real Internet address that points to a particular machine.

DoS

In a denial of service attack, many individual (usually compromised) computers are used to try and simultaneously access the same public resource with the intent of overburdening it so that it will not be able to adequately serve its normal users.

DOS

A disk operating system manages disks and other system resources. Sort of a subset of OSes, sort of an archaic term for the same. MS-DOS is the most popular program currently calling itself a DOS. CP/M was the most popular prior to MS-DOS.

download

To download a file is to copy it from a remote computer to your own. The opposite is upload.

DR-DOS

The DOS currently produced by Caldera (originally produced by Design Research as a successor to CP/M) designed to work like MS-DOS. While similar to CP/M in many ways, it utilizes simpler commands. It provides only a CLI, but either Windows 3.1 or GEOS may be run on top of it to provide a GUI. It only runs on x86 based machines.

driver

A driver is a piece of software that works with the OS to control a particular piece of hardware, like a printer or a scanner or a mouse or whatever.

DRM

Depending upon whom you ask, DRM can stand for either Digital Rights Management or Digital Restrictions Management. In either case, DRM is used to place restrictions upon the usage of digital media ranging from software to music to video.

DTML

The **D**ocument **T**emplate **M**ark-up **L**anguage is a subset of SGML and a superset of HTML used for creating documents that dynamically adapt to external conditions using its own custom tags and a little bit of Python. Note that it is quite different from the similarly named DHTML.

EDBIC

The EDBIC character set is similar to (but less popular than) the ASCII character set in concept, but is significantly different in layout. It tends to be found only on old machines..

emacs

Emacs is both one of the most powerful and one of the most popular text editing programs in existence. Versions can be found for most platforms, and in fact multiple companies make versions, so for a given platform there might even be a choice. There is even a free GNU version available. The drawback with emacs is that it is not in the least bit lightweight. In fact, it goes so far in the other direction that even its advocates will occasionally joke about it. It is however extremely capable. Almost anything that one would need to relating to text can be done with emacs and is probably built-in. Even if one manages to find something that emacs was not built to do, emacs has a built-in Lisp interpreter capable of not only extending its text editing capabilities, but even of being used as a scripting language in its own right.

embedded

An embedded system is a computer that lives inside another device and acts as a component of that device. For example, current cars have an embedded computer under the hood that helps regulate much of their day to day operation.

An embedded file is a file that lives inside another and acts as a portion of that file. This is frequently seen with HTML files having embedded audio files; audio files often embedded in HTML include AU files, MIDI files, SID files, WAV files, AIFF files, and MOD files. Most browsers will ignore these files unless an appropriate plug-in is present.

emulator

An emulator is a program that allows one computer platform to mimic another for the purposes of running its software. Typically (but not always) running a program through an emulator will not be quite as pleasant an experience as running it on the real system.

endian

A processor will be either "big endian" or "little endian" based upon the manner in which it encodes multiple byte values. There is no difference in performance between the two encoding methods, but it is one of the sources of difficulty when reading binary data on different platforms.

environment

An environment (sometimes also called a runtime environment) is a collection of external variable items or parameters that a program can access when run. Information about the computer's hardware and the user can often be found in the environment.

EPOC

EPOC is a lightweight OS. It is most commonly found on the Psion PDA.

extension

Filename extensions originate back in the days of CP/M and basically allow a very rough grouping of different file types by putting a tag at the end of the name. To further complicate matters, the tag is sometimes separated by the name proper by a period "." and sometimes by a tab. While extensions are semi-enforced on CP/M, MS-DOS, and MS-Windows, they have no real meaning aside from convention on other platforms and are only optional.

FAQ

A frequently asked questions file attempts to provide answers for all commonly asked questions related to a given topic.

FireWire

An incredibly fast type of serial port that offers many of the best features of SCSI at a lower price. Faster than most types of parallel port, a single FireWire port is capable of chaining many devices without the need of a terminator. FireWire is similar in many respects to USB but is significantly faster and somewhat more expensive. It is heavily used for connecting audio/video devices to computers, but is also used for connecting storage devices like drives and other assorted devices like printers and scanners.

fixed width

As applied to a font, fixed width means that every character takes up the same amount of space. That is, an "i" will be just as wide as an "m" with empty space being used for padding. The opposite is variable width. The most common fixed width font is Courier.

flash

Flash memory is similar to RAM. It has one significant advantage: it does not lose its contents when power is lost; it has two main disadvantages: it is slower, and it eventually wears out. Flash memory is frequently found in PCMCIA cards.

font

In a simplistic sense, a font can be thought of as the physical description of a character set. While the character set will define what sets of bits map to what letters, numbers, and other symbols, the font will define what each letter, number, and other symbol looks like. Fonts can be either fixed width or variable width and independently, either bitmapped or vectored. The size of the large characters in a font is typically measured in points.

Forth

A language developed in 1970 by Moore. Forth is fairly portable and has versions on many different platforms. While it is no longer an very popular language, many of its ideas and concepts have been carried into other computer programs. In particular, some programs for doing heavy-duty mathematical and engineering work use Forth-like interfaces.

FORTRAN

FORTRAN stands for **formula translation** and is the oldest computer language in the world. It is typically compiled and is quite fast. Its primary drawbacks are portability and ease-of-use -- often different FORTRAN compilers on different platforms behave quite differently in spite of standardization efforts in 1966 (FORTRAN 66 or FORTRAN IV), 1978 (FORTRAN 77), and 1991 (FORTRAN 90). Today languages like C and Java are more popular, but FORTRAN is still heavily used in military software. It is somewhat amusing to note that when FORTRAN was first released back in 1958 its advocates thought that it would mean the end of software bugs. In truth of course by making the creation of more complex software practical, computer languages have merely created new types of software bugs.

FreeBSD

A free variant of Berkeley UNIX available for Alpha and x86 based machines. It is not as popular as Linux.

freeware

Freeware is software that is available for free with no strings attached. The quality is often superb as the authors are also generally users.

FTP

The file transfer protocol is one of the most commonly used methods of copying files across the Internet. It has its origins on UNIX machines, but has been adapted to almost every type of computer in existence and is built into many browsers. Most FTP programs have two modes of operation, ASCII, and binary. Transmitting an ASCII file via the ASCII mode of operation is more efficient and cleaner. Transmitting a binary file via the ASCII mode of operation will result in a broken binary file. Thus the FTP programs that do not support both modes of operation will typically only do the binary mode, as binary transfers are capable of transferring both kinds of data without corruption.

gateway

A gateway connects otherwise separate computer networks.

GEOS

The **g**raphic **e**nvironment **o**perating **s**ystem is a lightweight OS with a GUI. It runs on several different processors, including the 65xx (different versions for different machines -- there are versions for the C64, the C128, and the Apple][, each utilizing the relevant custom chip sets), the x86 (although the x86 version is made to run on top of MS-DOS (or PC-DOS or DR-DOS) and is not strictly a full OS or a window manager, rather it is somewhat in between, like Windows 3.1) and numerous different PDAs, embedded devices, and hand-held machines. It was originally designed by Berkeley Softworks (no real relation to the Berkeley of UNIX fame) but is currently in a more interesting state: the company GeoWorks develops and promotes development of GEOS for hand-held devices, PDAs, & and embedded devices and owns (but has ceased further development on) the x86 version. The other versions are owned (and possibly still being developed) by the company CMD.

GHz & gigahertz

One gigahertz is equivalent to 1000 megahertz, or 1,000,000,000 hertz.

Glulx

A virtual machine optimized for running interactive fiction, interactive tutorials, and other interactive things of a primarily textual nature. Glulx has been ported to several platforms, and in in many ways an upgrade to the Z-machine.

GNOME

The **G**NU **n**etwork **o**bject **m**odel **e**nvironment is a popular free window manager (and much more -- as its name touts, it is more of a desktop environment) that runs under X-Windows. It is a part of the GNU project.

GNU

GNU stands for **GNU**'s **n**ot **U**NIX and is thus a recursive acronym (and unlike the animal name, the "G" here is pronounced). At any rate, the GNU project is an effort by the Free Software Foundation (FSF) to make all of the traditional UNIX utilities free for whoever wants them. The Free Software Foundation programmers know their stuff, and the quality of the GNU software is on par with the best produced commercially, and often better. All of the GNU software can be downloaded for free or obtained on CD-ROM for a small service fee. Documentation for all GNU software can be downloaded for free or obtained in book form for a small service fee. The Free Software Foundation pays its bills from the collection of service fees and the sale of T-shirts, and exists mostly through volunteer effort. It is based in Cambridge, MA.

gopher

Though not as popular as FTP or http, the gopher protocol is implemented by many browsers and numerous other programs and allows the transfer of files across networks. In some respects it can be thought of as a hybrid between FTP and http, although it tends not to be as good at raw file transfer as FTP and is not as flexible as http. The collection of documents available through gopher is often called "gopherspace", and it should be noted that gopherspace is older than the web. It should also be noted that gopher is not getting as much attention as it once did, and surfing through gopherspace is a little like exploring a ghost town, but there is an interesting VR interface available for it, and some things in gopherspace still have not been copied onto the web.

GUI

A **g**raphical **u**ser **i**nterface is a graphics-based means of communicating with a program, especially an OS or window manager. In fact, a window manager can be thought of as a GUI for a CLI OS.

HP-UX

HP-UX is the version of UNIX designed by Hewlett-Packard to work with their PA-RISC and

68xx based machines.

HTML

The **H**ypertext **M**ark-up **L**anguage is the language currently most frequently used to express web pages (although it is rapidly being replaced by XHTML). Every browser has the built-in ability to understand HTML. Some browsers can additionally understand Java and browse FTP areas. HTML is a proper subset of SGML.

http

The **h**ypertext **t**ransfer **p**rotocol is the native protocol of browsers and is most typically used to transfer HTML formatted files. The secure version is called "https".

Hurd

The Hurd is the official GNU OS. It is still in development and is not yet supported on too many different processors, but promises to be the most powerful OS available. It (like all the GNU software) is free.

Hz & hertz

Hertz means cycles per second, and makes no assumptions about what is cycling. So, for example, if a fluorescent light flickers once per jiffy, it has a 60 Hz flicker. More typical for computers would be a program that runs once per jiffy and thus has a 60 Hz frequency, or larger units of hertz like kHz, MHz, GHz, or THz.

i18n

Commonly used to abbreviate the word "internationalization". There are eighteen letters between the "i" and the "n". Similar to (and often used along with) i18n.

iCalendar

The iCalendar standard refers to the format used to store calendar type information (including events, to-do items, and journal entries) on the Internet. iCalendar data can be found on some World-Wide-Web pages or attached to e-mail messages.

icon

A small graphical display representing an object, action, or modifier of some sort.

IDE

Loosely speaking, a disk format sometimes used by MS-Windows, Mac OS, AmigaOS, and (rarely) UNIX. EIDE is enhanced IDE; it is much faster. Generally IDE is inferior (but less expensive) to SCSI, but it varies somewhat with system load and the individual IDE and SCSI components themselves. The quick rundown is that: SCSI-I and SCSI-II will almost always outperform IDE; EIDE will almost always outperform SCSI-I and SCSI-II; SCSI-III and UltraSCSI will almost always outperform EIDE; and heavy system loads give an advantage to SCSI. Note that although loosely speaking it is just a format difference, it is deep down a hardware difference.

Inform

A compiled, object-oriented language optimized for creating interactive fiction.

infrared communications

A device with an infrared port can communicate with other devices at a distance by beaming infrared light signals. Two incompatible protocols are used for infrared communications: IrDA and ASK. Many devices support both.

Instant Messenger

AOL's Instant Messenger is is a means of chatting over the Internet in real-time. It allows both open group discussions and private conversations. Instant Messenger uses a different, proprietary protocol from the more standard IRC, and is not supported on as many platforms.

interactive fiction

Interactive fiction (often abbreviated "IF" or "I-F") is a form of literature unique to the computer. While the reader cannot influence the direction of a typical story, the reader plays a more active role in an interactive fiction story and completely controls its direction. Interactive fiction works come in all the sizes and genres available to standard fiction, and in fact are not always even fiction per se (interactive tutorials exist and are slowly becoming more common).

interpreted

If a program is interpreted, its actual human-readable source is read as it is run by the computer. This is generally a slower process than if the program being run has already been compiled.

intranet

An intranet is a private network. There are many intranets scattered all over the world. Some are connected to the Internet via gateways.

IP

IP is the family of protocols that makes up the Internet. The two most common flavors are TCP/IP and UDP/IP.

IRC

Internet relay chat is a means of chatting over the Internet in real-time. It allows both open group discussions and private conversations. IRC programs are provided by many different companies and will work on many different platforms. AOL's Instant Messenger utilizes a separate incompatible protocol but is otherwise very similar.

IrDA

The Infrared Data Association (IrDA) is a voluntary organization of various manufacturers working together to ensure that the infrared communications between different computers, PDAs, printers, digital cameras, remote controls, etc. are all compatible with each other regardless of brand. The term is also often used to designate an IrDA compliant infrared communications port on a device. Informally, a device able to communicate via IrDA compliant infrared is sometimes simply said to "have IrDA". There is also an earlier, incompatible, and usually slower type of infrared communications still in use called ASK.

IRI

An Internationalized Resource Identifier is just a URI with i18n.

IRIX

The variant of UNIX designed by Silicon Graphics, Inc. IRIX machines are known for their graphics capabilities and were initially optimized for multimedia applications.

ISDN

An integrated service digital network line can be simply looked at as a digital phone line. ISDN connections to the Internet can be four times faster than the fastest regular phone connection, and because it is a digital connection a modem is not needed. Any computer hooked up to ISDN will typically require other special equipment in lieu of the modem, however. Also, both phone companies and ISPs charge more for ISDN connections than regular modem connections.

ISP

An Internet service provider is a company that provides Internet support for other entities. AOL (America Online) is a well-known ISP.

Java

A computer language designed to be both fairly lightweight and extremely portable. It is tightly bound to the web as it is the primary language for web applets. There has also been an OS based on Java for use on small hand-held, embedded, and network computers. It is called JavaOS. Java can be either interpreted or compiled. For web applet use it is almost always interpreted. While its interpreted form tends not to be very fast, its compiled form can often rival languages like C++ for speed. It is important to note however that speed is not Java's primary purpose -- raw speed is considered secondary to portabilty and ease of use.

JavaScript

JavaScript (in spite of its name) has nothing whatsoever to do with Java (in fact, it's arguably more like Newton Script than Java). JavaScript is an interpreted language built into a browser to provide a relatively simple means of adding interactivity to web pages. It is only supported on a few different browsers, and tends not to work exactly the same on different versions. Thus its use on the Internet is somewhat restricted to fairly simple programs. On intranets where there are usually fewer browser versions in use, JavaScript has been used to implement much more complex and impressive programs.

jiffy

A jiffy is 1/60 of a second. Jiffies are to seconds as seconds are to minutes.

joystick

A joystick is a physical device typically used to control objects on a computer screen. It is frequently used for games and sometimes used in place of a mouse.

JSON

The JSON is used for data interchange between programs, an area in which the ubiquitous XML is not too well-suited. JSON is lightweight and works extremely cleanly with languages languages including JavaScript, Python, Java, C++, and many others.

JSON-RPC

JSON-RPC is like XML-RPC but is significantly more lightweight since it uses JSON in lieu of XML.

KDE

The **K** desktop environment is a popular free window manager (and much more -- as its name touts, it is more of a desktop environment) that runs under X-Windows.

Kerberos

Kerberos is a network authentication protocol. Basically it preserves the integrity of passwords in any untrusted network (like the Internet). Kerberized applications work hand-in-hand with sites that support Kerberos to ensure that passwords cannot be stolen.

kernel

The very heart of an OS is often called its kernel. It will usually (at minimum) provide some libraries that give programmers access to its various features.

kHz & kilohertz

One kilohertz is equivalent to 1000 hertz. Some older computers have clock speeds measured in kHz.

l10n

Commonly used to abbreviate the word "localization". There are ten letters between the "l" and the "n". Similar to (and often used along with) i18n.

LDAP

The **L**ightweight **D**irectory **A**ccess **P**rotocol provides a means of sharing address book type of information across an intranet or even across the Internet. Note too that "address book type of information" here is pretty broad; it often includes not just human addresses, but machine addresses, printer configurations, and similar.

library

A selection of routines used by programmers to make computers do particular things.

lightweight

Something that is lightweight will not consume computer resources (such as RAM and disk space) too much and will thus run on less expensive computer systems.

Linux

Believe it or not, one of the fastest, most robust, and powerful multitasking OSes is available for free. Linux can be downloaded for free or be purchased on CD-ROM for a small service charge. A handful of companies distribute Linux including Red Hat, Debian, Caldera, and many others. Linux is also possibly available for more hardware combinations than any other OS (with the possible exception of NetBSD. Supported processors include: Alpha, PowerPC, SPARC, x86, and 68xx. Most processors currently not supported are currently works-in-progress or even available in beta. For example, work is currently underway to provide support for PA-RISC, 65xx, StrongARM, and Z80. People have even successfully gotten Linux working on PDAs. As you may have guessed, Linux can be made quite lightweight. Linux is a variant of UNIX and as such, most of the traditional UNIX software will run on Linux. This especially includes the GNU software, most of which comes with the majority of Linux distributions. Fast, reliable, stable, and inexpensive, Linux is popular with ISPs, software developers, and home hobbyists alike.

Lisp

Lisp stands for **lis**t processing and is the second oldest computer language in the world. Being developed in 1959, it lost the title to FORTRAN by only a few months. It is typically interpreted, but compilers are available for some platforms. Attempts were made to standardize the language, and the standard version is called "Common Lisp". There have also been efforts to simplify the language, and the results of these efforts is another language called Scheme. Lisp is a fairly portable language, but is not particularly fast. Today, Lisp is most widely used with AI software.

load

There are two popular meanings for load. The first means to fetch some data or a program from a disk and store it in memory. The second indicates the amount of work a component (especially a processor) is being made to do.

Logo

Logo is an interpreted language designed by Papert in 1966 to be a tool for helping people (especially kids) learn computer programming concepts. In addition to being used for that purpose, it is often used as a language for controlling mechanical robots and other similar devices. Logo interfaces even exist for building block / toy robot sets. Logo uses a special graphics cursor called "the turtle", and Logo is itself sometimes called "Turtle Graphics". Logo is quite portable but not particularly fast. Versions can be found on almost every computer platform in the world. Additionally, some other languages (notably some Pascal versions) provide Logo-like interfaces for graphics-intensive programming.

lossy

If a process is lossy, it means that a little quality is lost when it is performed. If a format is lossy, it means that putting data into that format (or possibly even manipulating it in that format) will cause some slight loss. Lossy processes and formats are typically used for performance or resource utilization reasons. The opposite of lossy is lossless.

Lua

Lua is a simple interpreted language. It is extremely portable, and free versions exist for most platforms.

Mac OS

Mac OS is the OS used on Macintosh computers. There are two distinctively different versions of it; everything prior to version 10 (sometimes called Mac OS Classic) and everything version 10 or later (called Mac OS X).

Mac OS Classic

The OS created by Apple and originally used by Macs is frequently (albeit slightly incorrectly) referred to as Mac OS Classic (officially Mac OS Classic is this original OS running under the modern Mac OS X in emulation. Mac OS combines the functionality of both an OS and a window manager and is often considered to be the easiest OS to use. It is partially multitasking but will still sometimes crash when dealing with a buggy program. It is probably the second most popular OS, next only to Windows 'XP (although it is quickly losing ground to Mac OS X) and has excellent driver support and boasts a fair selection of games. Mac OS will run on PowerPC and 68xx based machines.

Mac OS X

Mac OS X (originally called Rhapsody) is the industrial strength OS produced by Apple to run on both PowerPC and x86 systems (replacing what is often referred to as Mac OS Classic. Mac OS X is at its heart a variant of UNIX and possesses its underlying power (and the ability to run many of the traditional UNIX tools, including the GNU tools). It also was designed to mimic other OSes on demand via what it originally refered to as "boxes" (actually high-performance emulators); it has the built-in capability to run programs written for older Mac OS (via its "BlueBox", officially called Mac OS Classic) and work was started on making it also run Windows '95 / '98 / ME software (via what was called its "YellowBox"). There are also a few rumors going around that future versions may even be able to run Newton software (via the "GreenBox"). It provides a selection of two window managers built-in: Aqua and X-Windows (with Aqua being the default).

machine language

Machine language consists of the raw numbers that can be directly understood by a particular processor. Each processor's machine language will be different from other processors' machine language. Although called "machine language", it is not usually what people think of when talking about computer languages. Machine language dressed up with mnemonics to make it a bit more human-readable is called assembly language.

Macintosh

A Macintosh (or a Mac for short) is a computer system that has Mac OS for its OS. There are a few different companies that have produced Macs, but by far the largest is Apple. The oldest Macs are based on the 68xx processor; somewhat more recent Macs on the PowerPC processor, and current Macs on the x86 processor. The Macintosh was really the first general purpose computer to employ a GUI.

MacTel

An x86 based system running some flavor of Mac OS.

mainframe

A mainframe is any computer larger than a small piece of furniture. A modern mainframe is more powerful than a modern workstation, but more expensive and more difficult to maintain.

MathML

The **Math** **M**ark-up Language is a subset of XML used to represent mathematical formulae and equations. Typically it is found embedded within XHTML documents, although as of this writing not all popular browsers support it.

megahertz

A million cycles per second, abbreviated MHz. This is often used misleadingly to indicate processor speed, because while one might expect that a higher number would indicate a faster processor, that logic only holds true within a given type of processors as different types of processors are capable of doing different amounts of work within a cycle. For a current example, either a 200 MHz PowerPC or a 270 MHz SPARC will outperform a 300 MHz Pentium.

Merced

The Merced is a RISC processor developed by Intel with help from Hewlett-Packard and possibly Sun. It is just starting to be released, but is intended to eventually replace both the x86 and PA-RISC processors. Curiously, HP is recommending that everyone hold off using the first release and instead wait for the second one. It is expected some day to be roughly as fast as an Alpha or PowerPC. It is expected to be supported by future versions of Solaris, Windows-NT, HP-UX, Mac OS X, and Linux. The current semi-available Merced processor is called the Itanium. Its overall schedule is way behind, and some analysts predict that it never will really be released in significant quanitities.

MFM

Loosely speaking, An old disk format sometimes used by CP/M, MS-DOS, and MS-Windows. No longer too common as it cannot deliver close to the performance of either SCSI or IDE.

middleware

Software designed to sit in between an OS and applications. Common examples are Java and Tcl/Tk.

MIME

The **m**ulti-purpose **I**nternet **m**ail **e**xtensions specification describes a means of sending non-

ASCII data (such as images, sounds, foreign symbols, etc.) through e-mail. It commonly utilizes bcode.

MMX

Multimedia extensions were built into some x86 CPUs to provide better performance for certain operations, most notably graphics and sound. It is similar to AltiVec on the PowerPC CPUs. Like AltiVec, it requires special software for full performance benefits to be realized.

MOB

A **mo**vable **ob**ject is a graphical object that is manipulated separately from the background. These are seen all the time in computer games. When implemented in hardware, MOBs are sometimes called sprites.

Modula-2 & Modula-3

Modula-2 is a procedural language based on Pascal by its original author in around the 1977 - 1979 time period. Modula-3 is an intended successor that adds support for object-oriented constructs (among other things). Modula-2 can be either compiled or interpreted, while Modula-3 tends to be just a compiled language.

MOTD

A **m**essage **of** the **d**ay. Many computers (particularly more capable ones) are configured to display a MOTD when accessed remotely.

Motif

Motif is a popular commercial window manager that runs under X-Windows. Free work-alike versions are also available.

MS-DOS

The DOS produced by Microsoft. Early versions of it bear striking similarities to the earlier CP/M, but it utilizes simpler commands. It provides only a CLI, but either OS/2, Windows 3.1, Windows '95, Windows '98, Windows ME, or GEOS may be run on top of it to provide a GUI. It only runs on x86 based machines.

MS-Windows

MS-Windows is the name collectively given to several somewhat incompatible OSes all produced by Microsoft. They are: Windows CE, Windows NT, Windows 3.1, Windows '95, Windows '98, Windows ME, Windows 2000, and Windows XP.

MUD

A **mu**lti-**u**ser **d**imension (also sometimes called multi-user dungeon, but in either case abbreviated to "MUD") is sort of a combination between the online chatting abilities provided by something like IRC and a role-playing game. A MUD built with object oriented principles in mind is called a "Multi-user dimension object-oriented", or MOO. Yet another variant is called a "multi-user shell", or MUSH. Still other variants are called multi-user role-playing environments (MURPE) and multi-user environments (MUSE). There are probably more. In all cases the differences will be mostly academic to the regular user, as the same software is used to connect to all of them. Software to connect to MUDs can be found for most platforms, and there are even Java based ones that can run from within a browser.

multitasking

Some OSes have built into them the ability to do several things at once. This is called multitasking, and has been in use since the late sixties / early seventies. Since this ability is built into the software, the overall system will be slower running two things at once than it will be running just one thing. A system may have more than one processor built into it though, and such a system will be capable of running multiple things at once with less of a performance hit.

nagware

Nagware is a variant of shareware that will frequently remind its users to register.

NetBSD

A free variant of Berkeley UNIX available for Alpha, x86, 68xx, PA-RISC, SPARC, PowerPC, ARM, and many other types of machines. Its emphasis is on portability.

netiquette

The established conventions of online politeness are called netiquette. Some conventions vary from site to site or online medium to online medium; others are pretty standard everywhere. Newbies are often unfamiliar with the conventional rules of netiquette and sometimes embarrass themselves accordingly. Be sure not to send that incredibly important e-mail message before reading about netiquette.

newbie

A newbie is a novice to the online world or computers in general.

news

Usenet news can generally be thought of as public e-mail as that is generally the way it behaves. In reality, it is implemented by different software and is often accessed by different programs. Different newsgroups adhere to different topics, and some are "moderated", meaning that humans will try to manually remove off-topic posts, especially spam. Most established newsgroups have a FAQ, and people are strongly encouraged to read the FAQ prior to posting.

Newton

Although Newton is officially the name of the lightweight OS developed by Apple to run on its MessagePad line of PDAs, it is often used to mean the MessagePads (and compatible PDAs) themselves and thus the term "Newton OS" is often used for clarity. The Newton OS is remarkably powerful; it is fully multitasking in spite of the fact that it was designed for small machines. It is optimized for hand-held use, but will readily transfer data to all manner of desktop machines. Historically it was the first PDA. Recently Apple announced that it will discontinue further development of the Newton platform, but will instead work to base future hand-held devices on either Mac OS or Mac OS X with some effort dedicated to making the new devices capable of running current Newton programs.

Newton book

Newton books provide all the functionality of ordinary books but add searching and hypertext capabilities. The format was invented for the Newton to provide a means of making volumes of data portable, and is particularly popular in the medical community as most medical references are available as Newton books and carrying around a one pound Newton is preferable to carrying around twenty pounds of books, especially when it comes to looking up something. In addition to medical books, numerous references, most of the classics, and many contemporary works of fiction are available as Newton books. Most fiction is available for free, most references cost money. Newton books are somewhat more capable than the similar Palm DOC; both are specific types of e-books.

Newton Script

A intepreted, object-oriented language for Newton MessagePad computers.

nybble

A nybble is half a byte, or four bits. It is a case of computer whimsy; it only stands to reason that a small byte should be called a nybble. Some authors spell it with an "i" instead of the "y", but the "y" is the original form.

object-oriented

While the specifics are well beyond the scope of this document, the term "object-oriented" applies to a philosophy of software creation. Often this philosophy is referred to as object-oriented design (sometimes abbreviated as OOD), and programs written with it in mind are referred to as object-oriented programs (often abbreviated OOP). Programming languages designed to help facilitate it are called object-oriented languages (sometimes abbreviated as OOL) and databases built with it in mind are called object-oriented databases (sometimes abbreviated as OODB or less fortunately OOD). The general notion is that an object-oriented approach to creating software starts with modeling the real-world problems trying to be solved in familiar real-world ways, and carries the analogy all the way down to structure of the program. This is of course a great over-simplification. Numerous object-oriented programming languages exist including: Java, C++, Modula-2, Newton Script, and ADA.

Objective-C & ObjC

Objective-C (often called "ObjC" for short) is a compiled object-oriented language. Based heavily on C, Objective-C is nearly as fast and can often be thought of as being just C with added features. Note that it was developed independently of C++; its object-oriented extensions are more in the style of Smalltalk. It is however related to Objective-C++.

Objective-C++ & ObjC++

Objective-C++ (often called "ObjC++" for short) is a curious hybrid of Objective-C and C++, allowing the syntax of both to coexist in the same source files.

office suite

An office suite is a collection of programs including at minimum a word processor, spreadsheet, drawing program, and minimal database program. Some common office suites include MS-Office, AppleWorks, ClarisWorks, GeoWorks, Applixware, Corel Office, and StarOffice.

open source

Open source software goes one step beyond freeware. Not only does it provide the software for free, it provides the original source code used to create the software. Thus, curious users can poke around with it to see how it works, and advanced users can modify it to make it work better for them. By its nature, open souce software is pretty well immune to all types of computer virus.

OpenBSD

A free variant of Berkeley UNIX available for Alpha, x86, 68xx, PA-RISC, SPARC, and PowerPC based machines. Its emphasis is on security.

OpenDocument & ODF

OpenDocument (or ODF for short) is the suite of open, XML-based office suite application formats defined by the OASIS consortium. It defines a platform-neutral, non-proprietary way of storing documents.

OpenGL

A low-level 3D graphics library with an emphasis on speed developed by SGI.

OS/2

OS/2 is the OS designed by IBM to run on x86 based machines. It is semi-compatible with MS-Windows. IBM's more industrial strength OS is called AIX.

PA-RISC

The PA-RISC is a RISC processor developed by Hewlett-Packard. It is currently produced only by HP. At the moment only one OS runs on PA-RISC based machines: HP-UX. There is an effort underway to port Linux to them, though.

Palm DOC

Palm DOC files are quite similar to (but slightly less capable than) Newton books. They were designed for Palm Pilots but can now be read on a couple other platforms, too. They are a specific type of e-book.

Palm Pilot

The Palm Pilot (also called both just Palm and just Pilot, officially now just Palm) is the most popular PDA currently in use. It is one of the least capable PDAs, but it is also one of the smallest and least expensive. While not as full featured as many of the other PDAs (such as the Newton) it performs what features it does have quite well and still remains truly pocket-sized.

parallel

Loosely speaking, parallel implies a situation where multiple things can be done simultaneously, like having multiple check-out lines each serving people all at once. Parallel connections are by their nature more expensive than serial ones, but usually faster. Also, in a related use of the word, often multitasking computers are said to be capable of running multiple programs in parallel.

partition

Sometimes due to hardware limitations, disks have to be divided into smaller pieces. These

24

pieces are called partitions.

Pascal

Named after the mathematician Blaise Pascal, Pascal is a language designed by Niklaus Wirth originally in 1968 (and heavily revised in 1972) mostly for purposes of education and training people how to write computer programs. It is a typically compiled language but is still usually slower than C or FORTRAN. Wirth also created a more powerful object-oriented Pascal-like language called Modula-2.

PC-DOS

The DOS produced by IBM designed to work like MS-DOS. Early versions of it bear striking similarities to the earlier CP/M, but it utilizes simpler commands. It provides only a CLI, but either Windows 3.1 or GEOS may be run on top of it to provide a GUI. It only runs on x86 based machines.

PCMCIA

The **P**ersonal **C**omputer **M**emory **C**ard **I**nternational **A**ssociation is a standards body that concern themselves with PC Card technology. Often the PC Cards themselves are referred to as "PCMCIA cards". Frequently flash memory can be found in PC card form.

Perl

Perl is an interpreted language extremely popular for web applications.

PET

The Commodore PET (**P**ersonal **E**lectronic **T**ransactor) is an early (circa 1977-1980, around the same time as the Apple][) home computer featuring a ROM-based BASIC developed by Microsoft which it uses as a default "OS". It is based on the 65xx family of processors and is the precursor to the VIC-20.

PETSCII

The PETSCII character set gets its name from "**PET** ASCII; it is a variant of the ASCII character set originally developed for the Commodore PET that swaps the upper and lower case characters and adds over a hundred graphic characters in addition to other small changes. If you encounter some text that seems to have uppercase where lowercase is expected and vice-versa, it is probably a PETSCII file.

PHP

Named with a recursive acronym (PHP: Hypertext Preprocessor), PHP provides a means of creating web pages that dynamically modify themselves on the fly.

ping

Ping is a protocol designed to check across a network to see if a particular computer is "alive" or not. Computers that recognize the ping will report back their status. Computers that are down will not report back anything at all.

pixel

The smallest distinct point on a computer display is called a pixel.

plug-in

A plug-in is a piece of software designed not to run on its own but rather work in cooperation with a separate application to increase that application's abilities.

point

There are two common meanings for this word. The first is in the geometric sense; a position in space without size. Of course as applied to computers it must take up some space in practise (even if not in theory) and it is thus sometimes synonomous with pixel. The other meaning is related most typically to fonts and regards size. The exact meaning of it in this sense will unfortunately vary somewhat from person to person, but will often mean 1/72 of an inch. Even when it does not exactly mean 1/72 of an inch, larger point sizes always indicate larger fonts.

PowerPC

The PowerPC is a RISC processor developed in a collaborative effort between IBM, Apple, and Motorola. It is currently produced by a few different companies, of course including its original

25

developers. A few different OSes run on PowerPC based machines, including Mac OS, AIX, Solaris, Windows NT, Linux, Mac OS X, BeOS, and AmigaOS. At any given time, the fastest processor in the world is usually either a PowerPC or an Alpha, but sometimes SPARCs and PA-RISCs make the list, too.

proprietary

This simply means to be supplied by only one vendor. It is commonly misused. Currently, most processors are non-proprietary, some systems are non-proprietary, and every OS (except for arguably Linux) is proprietary.

protocol

A protocol is a means of communication used between computers. As long as both computers recognize the same protocol, they can communicate without too much difficulty over the same network or even via a simple direct modem connection regardless whether or not they are themselves of the same type. This means that WinTel boxes, Macs, Amigas, UNIX machines, etc., can all talk with one another provided they agree on a common protocol first.

Psion

The Psion is a fairly popular brand of PDA. Generally, it is in between a Palm and a Newton in capability. It runs the EPOC OS.

Python

Python is an interpreted, object-oriented language popular for Internet applications. It is extremely portable with free versions existing for virtually every platform.

queue

A queue is a waiting list of things to be processed. Many computers provide printing queues, for example. If something is being printed and the user requests that another item be printed, the second item will sit in the printer queue until the first item finishes printing at which point it will be removed from the queue and get printed itself.

QuickDraw

A high-level 3D graphics library with an emphasis on quick development time created by Apple.

RAM

Random access memory is the short-term memory of a computer. Any information stored in RAM will be lost if power goes out, but the computer can read from RAM far more quickly than from a drive.

random access

Also called "dynamic access" this indicates that data can be selected without having to skip over earlier data first. This is the way that a CD, record, laserdisc, or DVD will behave -- it is easy to selectively play a particular track without having to fast forward through earlier tracks. The other common behavior is called sequential access.

RDF

The Resource Description Framework is built upon an XML base and provides a more modern means of accessing data from Internet resources. It can provide metadata (including annotations) for web pages making (among other things) searching more capable. It is also being used to refashion some existing formats like RSS and iCalendar; in the former case it is already in place (at least for newer RSS versions), but it is still experimental in the latter case.

real-time

Something that happens in real-time will keep up with the events around it and never give any sort of "please wait" message.

Rexx

The Restructured Extended Executor is an interpreted language designed primarily to be embedded in other applications in order to make them consistently programmable, but also to be easy to learn and understand.

RISC

Reduced instruction set computing is one of the two main types of processor design in use today, the other being CISC. The fastest processors in the world today are all RISC designs. There are several popular RISC processors, including Alphas, ARMs, PA-RISCs, PowerPCs, and SPARCs.

robot

A robot (or 'bot for short) in the computer sense is a program designed to automate some task, often just sending messages or collecting information. A spider is a type of robot designed to traverse the web performing some task (usually collecting data).

robust

The adjective robust is used to describe programs that are better designed, have fewer bugs, and are less likely to crash.

ROM

Read-only memory is similar to RAM only cannot be altered and does not lose its contents when power is removed.

RSS

RSS stands for either **R**ich **S**ite **S**ummary, **R**eally **S**imple **S**yndication, or **R**DF **S**ite **S**ummary, depending upon whom you ask. The general idea is that it can provide brief summaries of articles that appear in full on a web site. It is well-formed XML, and newer versions are even more specifically well-formed RDF.

Ruby

Ruby is an interpreted, object-oriented language. Ruby was fairly heavily influenced by Perl, so people familiar with that language can typically transition to Ruby easily.

scanner

A scanner is a piece of hardware that will examine a picture and produce a computer file that represents what it sees. A digital camera is a related device. Each has its own limitations.

Scheme

Scheme is a typically interpreted computer language. It was created in 1975 in an attempt to make Lisp simpler and more consistent. Scheme is a fairly portable language, but is not particularly fast.

script

A script is a series of OS commands. The term "batch file" means much the same thing, but is a bit dated. Typically the same sort of situations in which one would say DOS instead of OS, it would also be appropriate to say batch file instead of script. Scripts can be run like programs, but tend to perform simpler tasks. When a script is run, it is always interpreted.

SCSI

Loosely speaking, a disk format sometimes used by MS-Windows, Mac OS, AmigaOS, and (almost always) UNIX. Generally SCSI is superior (but more expensive) to IDE, but it varies somewhat with system load and the individual SCSI and IDE components themselves. The quick rundown is that: SCSI-I and SCSI-II will almost always outperform IDE; EIDE will almost always outperform SCSI-I and SCSI-II; SCSI-III and UltraSCSI will almost always outperform EIDE; and heavy system loads give an advantage to SCSI. Note that although loosely speaking it is just a format difference, it is deep down a hardware difference.

sequential access

This indicates that data cannot be selected without having to skip over earlier data first. This is the way that a cassette or video tape will behave. The other common behavior is called random access.

serial

Loosely speaking, serial implies something that has to be done linearly, one at a time, like people being served in a single check-out line. Serial connections are by their nature less expensive than parallel connections (including things like SCSI) but are typically slower.

server

A server is a computer designed to provide various services for an entire network. It is typically either a workstation or a mainframe because it will usually be expected to handle far greater loads than ordinary desktop systems. The load placed on servers also necessitates that they utilize robust OSes, as a crash on a system that is currently being used by many people is far worse than a crash on a system that is only being used by one person.

SGML

The **S**tandard **G**eneralized **M**ark-up **L**anguage provides an extremely generalized level of mark-up. More common mark-up languages like HTML and XML are actually just popular subsets of SGML.

shareware

Shareware is software made for profit that allows a trial period before purchase. Typically shareware can be freely downloaded, used for a period of weeks (or sometimes even months), and either purchased or discarded after it has been learned whether or not it will satisfy the user's needs.

shell

A CLI designed to simplify complex OS commands. Some OSes (like AmigaOS, the Hurd, and UNIX) have built-in support to make the concurrent use of multiple shells easy. Common shells include the Korn Shell (ksh), the Bourne Shell (sh or bsh), the Bourne-Again Shell, (bash or bsh), the C-Shell (csh), etc.

SIMM

A physical component used to add RAM to a computer. Similar to, but incompatible with, DIMMs.

Smalltalk

Smalltalk is an efficient language for writing computer programs. Historically it is one of the first object-oriented languages, and is not only used today in its pure form but shows its influence in other languages like Objective-C.

Solaris

Solaris is the commercial variant of UNIX currently produced by Sun. It is an industrial strength, nigh bulletproof, powerful multitasking OS that will run on SPARC, x86, and PowerPC based machines.

spam

Generally spam is unwanted, unrequested e-mail or Usenet news. It is typically sent out in bulk to huge address lists that were automatically generated by various robots endlessly searching the Internet and newsgroups for things that resemble e-mail addresses. The legality of spam is a topic of much debate; it is at best only borderline legal, and spammers have been successfully persecuted in some states.

SPARC

The SPARC is a RISC processor developed by Sun. The design was more or less released to the world, and it is currently produced by around a dozen different companies too numerous to even bother mentioning. It is worth noting that even computers made by Sun typically sport SPARCs made by other companies. A couple different OSes run on SPARC based machines, including Solaris, SunOS, and Linux. Some of the newer SPARC models are called UltraSPARCs.

sprite

The term sprite originally referred to a small MOB, usually implemented in hardware. Lately it is also being used to refer to a single image used piecemeal within a Web site in order to avoid incurring the time penalty of downloading multiple files.

SQL

SQL (pronounced **Sequel**) is an interpreted language specially designed for database access. It is supported by virtually every major modern database system.

Sugar

The window manager used by the OLPC XO. It is made to run on top of Linux.

SunOS

SunOS is the commercial variant of UNIX formerly produced (but still supported) by Sun.

SVG

Scalable Vector Graphics data is an XML file that is used to hold graphical data that can be resized without loss of quality. SVG data can be kept in its own file, or even embedded within a web page (although not all browsers are capable of displaying such data).

Tcl/Tk

The Tool Command Language is a portable interpreted computer language designed to be easy to use. Tk is a GUI toolkit for Tcl. Tcl is a fairly popular language for both integrating existing applications and for creating Web applets (note that applets written in Tcl are often called Tcklets). Tcl/Tk is available for free for most platforms, and plug-ins are available to enable many browsers to play Tcklets.

TCP/IP

TCP/IP is a protocol for computer networks. The Internet is largely built on top of TCP/IP (it is the more reliable of the two primary Internet Protocols -- TCP stands for **T**ransmission **C**ontrol **P**rotocol).

terminator

A terminator is a dedicated device used to mark the end of a device chain (as is most typically found with SCSI devices). If such a chain is not properly terminated, weird results can occur.

TEX

TEX (pronounced "tek") is a freely available, industrial strength typesetting program that can be run on many different platforms. These qualities make it exceptionally popular in schools, and frequently software developed at a university will have its documentation in TEX format. TEX is not limited to educational use, though; many professional books were typeset with TEX. TEX's primary drawback is that it can be quite difficult to set up initially.

THz & terahertz

One terahertz is equivalent to 1000 gigahertz.

TrackBack

TrackBacks essentially provide a means whereby different web sites can post messages to one another not just to inform each other about citations, but also to alert one another of related resources. Typically, a blog may display quotations from another blog through the use of TrackBacks.

UDP/IP

UDP/IP is a protocol for computer networks. It is the faster of the two primary Internet **P**rotocols. UDP stands for **U**ser **D**atagram **P**rotocol.

Unicode

The Unicode character set is a superset of the ASCII character set with provisions made for handling international symbols and characters from other languages. Unicode is sixteen bit, so takes up roughly twice the space as simple ASCII, but is correspondingly more flexible.

UNIX

UNIX is a family of OSes, each being made by a different company or organization but all offering a very similar look and feel. It can not quite be considered non-proprietary, however, as the differences between different vendor's versions can be significant (it is still generally possible to switch from one vendor's UNIX to another without too much effort; today the differences between different UNIXes are similar to the differences between the different MS-Windows; historically there were two different UNIX camps, Berkeley / BSD and AT&T / System V, but the assorted vendors have worked together to minimalize the differences). The free variant Linux is one of the closest things to a current, non-proprietary OS; its development is controlled by a non-profit organization and its distribution is provided by several companies. UNIX is powerful; it is fully multitasking and can do pretty much anything that any OS can do (look to the Hurd if you need a more powerful OS). With power comes complexity, however, and

UNIX tends not to be overly friendly to beginners (although those who think UNIX is difficult or cryptic apparently have not used CP/M). Window managers are available for UNIX (running under X-Windows) and once properly configured common operations will be almost as simple on a UNIX machine as on a Mac. Out of all the OSes in current use, UNIX has the greatest range of hardware support. It will run on machines built around many different processors. Lightweight versions of UNIX have been made to run on PDAs, and in the other direction, full featured versions make full advantage of all the resources on large, multi-processor machines. Some different UNIX versions include Solaris, Linux, IRIX, AIX, SunOS, FreeBSD, Digital UNIX, HP-UX, NetBSD, OpenBSD, etc.

upload

To upload a file is to copy it from your computer to a remote computer. The opposite is download.

UPS

An uninterrupted power supply uses heavy duty batteries to help smooth out its input power source.

URI

A **U**niform **R**esource **I**dentifier is basically just a unique address for almost any type of resource. It is similar to but more general than a URL; in fact, it may also be a URN.

URL

A **U**niform **R**esource **L**ocator is basically just an address for a file that can be given to a browser. It starts with a protocol type (such as http, ftp, or gopher) and is followed by a colon, machine name, and file name in UNIX style. Optionally an octothorpe character "#" and and arguments will follow the file name; this can be used to further define position within a page and perform a few other tricks. Similar to but less general than a URI.

URN

A **U**niform **R**esource **N**ame is basically just a unique address for almost any type of resource unlike a URL it will probably not resolve with a browser.

USB

A really fast type of serial port that offers many of the best features of SCSI without the price. Faster than many types of parallel port, a single USB port is capable of chaining many devices without the need of a terminator. USB is much slower (but somewhat less expensive) than FireWire.

uucode

The point of uucode is to allow 8-bit binary data to be transferred through the more common 7-bit ASCII channels (most especially e-mail). The facilities for dealing with uucoded files exist for many different machine types, and the most common programs are called "uuencode" for encoding the original binary file into a 7-bit file and "uudecode" for restoring the original binary file from the encoded one. Sometimes different uuencode and uudecode programs will work in subtly different manners causing annoying compatibility problems. Bcode was invented to provide the same service as uucode but to maintain a tighter standard.

variable width

As applied to a font, variable width means that different characters will have different widths as appropriate. For example, an "i" will take up much less space than an "m". The opposite of variable width is fixed width. The terms "proportional width" and "proportionally spaced" mean the same thing as variable width. Some common variable width fonts include Times, Helvetica, and Bookman.

VAX

The VAX is a computer platform developed by Digital. Its plural is VAXen. VAXen are large expensive machines that were once quite popular in large businesses; today modern UNIX workstations have all the capability of VAXen but take up much less space. Their OS is called VMS.

vector

This term has two common meanings. The first is in the geometric sense: a vector defines a direction and magnitude. The second concerns the formatting of fonts and images. If a font is a vector font or an image is a vector image, it is defined as lines of relative size and direction rather than as collections of pixels (the method used in bitmapped fonts and images). This makes it easier to change the size of the font or image, but puts a bigger load on the device that has to display the font or image. The term "outline font" means the same thing as vector font.

Veronica & Veronica2

Although traditionally written as a proper name, Veronica is actually an acronym for "**v**ery **e**asy **r**odent-**o**riented **n**etwide **i**ndex to **c**omputerized **a**rchives", where the "rodent" refers to gopher. The acronym was obviously a little forced to go along with the pre-existing (and now largely unused) Archie, in order to have a little fun with a comic book reference. Regardless, Veronica (or these days more likely Veronica2) is essentially a search engine for gopher resources.

VIC-20

The Commodore VIC-20 computer sold millions of units and is generally considered to have been the first affordable home computer. It features a ROM-based BASIC and uses it as a default "OS". It is based on the 65xx family of processors. VIC (in case you are wondering) can stand for either **v**ideo **i**nterface **c** or **v**ideo **i**nterface **c**omputer. The VIC-20 is the precursor to the C64/128.

virtual machine

A virtual machine is a machine completely defined and implemented in software rather than hardware. It is often referred to as a "runtime environment"; code compiled for such a machine is typically called bytecode.

virtual memory

This is a scheme by which disk space is made to substitute for the more expensive RAM space. Using it will often enable a comptuer to do things it could not do without it, but it will also often result in an overall slowing down of the system. The concept of swap space is very similar.

virtual reality

Virtual reality (often called VR for short) is generally speaking an attempt to provide more natural, human interfaces to software. It can be as simple as a pseudo 3D interface or as elaborate as an isolated room in which the computer can control the user's senses of vision, hearing, and even smell and touch.

virus

A virus is a program that will seek to duplicate itself in memory and on disks, but in a subtle way that will not immediately be noticed. A computer on the same network as an infected computer or that uses an infected disk (even a floppy) or that downloads and runs an infected program can itself become infected. A virus can only spread to computers of the same platform. For example, on a network consisting of a WinTel box, a Mac, and a Linux box, if one machine acquires a virus the other two will probably still be safe. Note also that different platforms have different general levels of resistance; UNIX machines are almost immune, Win '95 / '98 / ME / XP is quite vulnerable, and most others lie somewhere in between.

VMS

The industrial strength OS that runs on VAXen.

VoIP

VoIP means "Voice over IP" and it is quite simply a way of utilizing the Internet (or even in some cases intranets) for telephone conversations. The primary motivations for doing so are cost and convenience as VoIP is significantly less expensive than typical telephone long distance packages, plus one high speed Internet connection can serve for multiple phone lines.

VRML

A **V**irtual **R**eality **M**odeling **L**anguage file is used to represent VR objects. It has essentially been superceded by X3D.

W3C

The World Wide Web Consortium (usually abbreviated W3C) is a non-profit, advisory body that makes suggestions on the future direction of the World Wide Web, HTML, CSS, and browsers.

Waba

An extremely lightweight subset of Java optimized for use on PDAs.

WebDAV

WebDAV stands for Web-based Distributed Authoring and Versioning, and is designed to provide a way of editing Web-based resources in place. It serves as a more modern (and often more secure) replacement for FTP in many cases.

WebTV

A WebTV box hooks up to an ordinary television set and displays web pages. It will not display them as well as a dedicated computer.

window manager

A window manager is a program that acts as a graphical go-between for a user and an OS. It provides a GUI for the OS. Some OSes incorporate the window manager into their own internal code, but many do not for reasons of efficiency. Some OSes partially make the division. Some common true window managers include CDE (Common Desktop Environment), GNOME, KDE, Aqua, OpenWindows, Motif, FVWM, Sugar, and Enlightenment. Some common hybrid window managers with OS extensions include Windows ME, Windows 98, Windows 95, Windows 3.1, OS/2 and GEOS.

Windows '95

Windows '95 is currently the second most popular variant of MS-Windows. It was designed to be the replacement Windows 3.1 but has not yet done so completely partly because of suspected security problems but even more because it is not as lightweight and will not work on all the machines that Windows 3.1 will. It is more capable than Windows 3.1 though and now has excellent driver support and more games available for it than any other platform. It is made to run on top of MS-DOS and will not do much of anything if MS-DOS is not on the system. It is thus not strictly an OS per se, but nor is it a true window manager either; rather the combination of MS-DOS and Windows '95 result in a full OS with GUI. It is partially multitasking but has a much greater chance of crashing than Windows NT does (or probably even Mac OS) if faced with a buggy program. Windows '95 runs only on x86 based machines. Currently Windows '95 has several Y2K issues, some of which have patches that can be downloaded for free, and some of which do not yet have fixes at all.

Windows '98

Windows '98 is quite possibly the second most popular form of MS-Windows, in spite of the fact that its official release is currently a point of legal debate with at least nineteen states, the federal government, and a handful of foreign countries as it has a few questionable features that might restrict the novice computer user and/or unfairly compete with other computer companies. It also has some specific issues with the version of Java that comes prepackaged with it that has never been adequately fixed, and it still has several Y2K issues, most of which have patches that can be downloaded for free (in fact, Microsoft guarantees that it will work properly through 2000 with the proper patches), but some of which do not yet have fixes at all (it won't work properly through 2001 at this point). In any case, it was designed to replace Windows '95.

Windows 2000

Windows 2000 was the intended replacement for Windows NT and in that capacity received relatively lukewarm support. Being based on Windows NT, it inherits some of its driver support problems. Originally it was also supposed to replace Windows '98, but Windows ME was made to do that instead, and the merger between Windows NT and Windows '98 was postponed until Windows XP.

Windows 3.1

Windows 3.1 remains a surprisingly popular variant of MS-Windows. It is lighter weight than either Windows '95 or Windows NT (but not lighter weight than GEOS) but less capable than the other two. It is made to run on top of MS-DOS and will not do much of anything if MS-DOS is not on the system. It is thus not strictly an OS per se, but nor is it a true window manager, either; rather the combination of MS-DOS and Windows 3.1 result in a full OS with GUI. Its driver support is good, but its game selection is limited. Windows 3.1 runs only on x86 based machines. It has some severe Y2K issues that may or may not be fixed.

Windows CE

Windows CE is the lightweight variant of MS-Windows. It offers the general look and feel of Windows '95 but is targetted primarily for hand-held devices, PDAs, NCs, and embedded devices. It does not have all the features of either Windows '95 or Windows NT and is very different from Windows 3.1. In particular, it will not run any software made for any of the other versions of MS-Windows. Special versions of each program must be made. Furthermore, there are actually a few slightly different variants of Windows CE, and no variant is guaranteed to be able to run software made specifically for another one. Driver support is also fairly poor for all types, and few games are made for it. Windows CE will run on a few different processor types, including the x86 and several different processors dedicated to PDAs, embedded systems, and hand-held devices.

Windows ME

Windows ME is yet another flavor of MS-Windows (specifically the planned replacement for Windows '98). Windows ME currently runs only on the x86 processor.

Windows NT

Windows NT is the industrial-strength variant of MS-Windows. Current revisions offer the look and feel of Windows '95 and older revisions offer the look and feel of Windows 3.1. It is the most robust flavor of MS-Windows and is fully multitasking. It is also by far the most expensive flavor of MS-Windows and has far less software available for it than Windows '95 or '98. In particular, do not expect to play many games on a Windows NT machine, and expect some difficulty in obtaining good drivers. Windows NT will run on a few different processor types, including the x86, the Alpha, and the PowerPC. Plans are in place to port Windows NT to the Merced when it becomes available.

Windows Vista

Windows Vista is the newest flavor of MS-Windows (specifically the planned replacement for Windows XP). Windows Vista (originally known as Longhorn) currently only runs on x86 processors.

Windows XP

Windows XP is yet another flavor of MS-Windows (specifically the planned replacement for both Windows ME and Windows 2000). Windows XP currently only runs on the x86 processors. Windows XP is currently the most popular form of MS-Windows.

WinTel

An x86 based system running some flavor of MS-Windows.

workstation

Depending upon whom you ask, a workstation is either an industrial strength desktop computer or its own category above the desktops. Workstations typically have some flavor of UNIX for their OS, but there has been a recent trend to call high-end Windows NT and Windows 2000 machines workstations, too.

WYSIWYG

What you see is what you get; an adjective applied to a program that attempts to exactly represent printed output on the screen. Related to WYSIWYM but quite different.

WYSIWYM

What you see is what you mean; an adjective applied to a program that does not attempt to exactly represent printed output on the screen, but rather defines how things are used and so will adapt to different paper sizes, etc. Related to WYSIWYG but quite different.

X-Face

X-Faces are small monochrome images embedded in headers for both provides a e-mail and news messages. Better mail and news applications will display them (sometimes automatically, sometimes only per request).

X-Windows

X-Windows provides a GUI for most UNIX systems, but can also be found as an add-on library for other computers. Numerous window managers run on top of it. It is often just called "X".

X3D

Extensible **3D** Graphics data is an XML file that is used to hold three-dimensional graphical data. It is the successor to VRML.

x86

The x86 series of processors includes the Pentium, Pentium Pro, Pentium II, Pentium III, Celeron, and Athlon as well as the 786, 686, 586, 486, 386, 286, 8086, 8088, etc. It is an exceptionally popular design (by far the most popular CISC series) in spite of the fact that even its fastest model is significantly slower than the assorted RISC processors. Many different OSes run on machines built around x86 processors, including MS-DOS, Windows 3.1, Windows '95, Windows '98, Windows ME, Windows NT, Windows 2000, Windows CE, Windows XP, GEOS, Linux, Solaris, OpenBSD, NetBSD, FreeBSD, Mac OS X, OS/2, BeOS, CP/M, etc. A couple different companies produce x86 processors, but the bulk of them are produced by Intel. It is expected that this processor will eventually be completely replaced by the Merced, but the Merced development schedule is somewhat behind. Also, it should be noted that the Pentium III processor has stirred some controversy by including a "fingerprint" that will enable individual computer usage of web pages etc. to be accurately tracked.

XBL

An XML Binding Language document is used to associate executable content with an XML tag. It is itself an XML file, and is used most frequently (although not exclusively) in conjunction with XUL.

XHTML

The Extensible **H**ypertext **M**ark-up **L**anguage is essentially a cleaner, stricter version of HTML. It is a proper subset of XML.

XML

The Extensible **M**ark-up **L**anguage is a subset of SGML and a superset of XHTML. It is used for numerous things including (among many others) RSS and RDF.

XML-RPC

XML-RPC provides a fairly lightweight means by which one computer can execute a program on a co-operating machine across a network like the Internet. It is based on XML and is used for everything from fetching stock quotes to checking weather forcasts.

XO

The energy-efficient, kid-friendly laptop produced by the OLPC project. It runs Sugar for its window manager and Linux for its OS. It sports numerous built-in features like wireless networking, a video camera & microphone, a few USB ports, and audio in/out jacks. It comes with several educational applications (which it refers to as "Activities"), most of which are written in Python.

XSL

The Extensible Stylesheet Language is like CSS for XML. It provides a means of describing how an XML resource should be displayed.

XSLT

XSL Transformations are used to transform one type of XML into another. It is a component of XSL that can be (and often is) used independently.

XUL

An XML User-Interface Language document is used to define a user interface for an application using XML to specify the individual controls as well as the overall layout.

Y2K

The general class of problems resulting from the wrapping of computers' internal date timers is given this label in honor of the most obvious occurrence -- when the year changes from 1999 to 2000 (abbreviated in some programs as 99 to 00 indicating a backwards time movement). Contrary to popular belief, these problems will not all manifest themselves on the first day of 2000, but will in fact happen over a range of dates extending out beyond 2075. A computer that does not have problems prior to the beginning of 2001 is considered "Y2K compliant", and a computer that does not have problems within the next ten years or so is considered for all practical purposes to be "Y2K clean". Whether or not a given computer is "clean" depends upon both its OS and its applications (and in some unfortunate cases, its hardware). The quick rundown on common home / small business machines (roughly from best to worst) is that:

All Mac OS systems are okay until at least the year 2040. By that time a patch should be available.

All BeOS systems are okay until the year 2040 (2038?). By that time a patch should be available.

Most UNIX versions are either okay or currently have free fixes available (and typically would not have major problems until 2038 or later in any case).

NewtonOS has a problem with the year 2010, but has a free fix available.

Newer AmigaOS systems are okay; older ones have a problem with the year 2000 but have a free fix available. They also have a year 2077 problem that does not yet have a free fix.

Some OS/2 systems have a year 2000 problem, but free fixes are available.

All CP/M versions have a year 2000 problem, but free fixes are available.

PC-DOS has a year 2000 problem, but a free fix is available.

DR-DOS has a year 2000 problem, but a free fix is available.

Different versions of GEOS have different problems ranging from minor year 2000 problems (with fixes in the works) to larger year 2080 problems (that do not have fixes yet). The only problem that may not have a fix in time is the year 2000 problem on the Apple][version of GEOS; not only was that version discontinued, unlike the other GEOS versions it no longer has a parent company to take care of it.

All MS-Windows versions (except possibly Windows 2000 and Windows ME) have multiple problems with the year 2000 and/or 2001, most of which have free fixes but some of which still lack free fixes as of this writing. Even new machines off the shelf that are labelled "Y2K Compliant" usually are not unless additional software is purchased and installed. Basically WinNT and WinCE can be properly patched, Windows '98 can be patched to work properly through 2000 (possibly not 2001), Windows '95 can be at least partially patched for 2000 (but not 2001) but is not being guaranteed by Microsoft, and Windows 3.1 cannot be fully patched.

MS-DOS has problems with at least the year 2000 (and probably more). None of its problems have been addressed as of this writing. Possible fixes are to change over to either PC-DOS or DR-DOS.

Results vary wildly for common applications, so it is better to be safe than sorry and check out the ones that you use. It should also be noted that some of the biggest expected Y2K problems will be at the two ends of the computer spectrum with older legacy mainframes (such as power some large banks) and some of the various tiny embedded computers (such as power most burglar alarms and many assorted appliances). Finally, it should also be mentioned that some older WinTel boxes and Amigas may have Y2K problems in their hardware requiring a card addition or replacement.

Z-Machine

A virtual machine optimized for running interactive fiction, interactive tutorials, and other interactive things of a primarily textual nature. Z-Machines have been ported to almost every platform in use today. Z-machine bytecode is usually called Z-code. The Glulx virtual machine is of the same idea but somewhat more modern in concept.

Z80

The Z80 series of processors is a CISC design and is not being used in too many new stand-alone computer systems, but can still be occasionally found in embedded systems. It is the most popular processor for CP/M machines.

Zaurus

The Zaurus is a brand of PDA. It is generally in between a Palm and a Newton in capability.

zip

There are three common zips in the computer world that are completely different from one another. One is a type of removable removable disk slightly larger (physically) and vastly larger (capacity) than a floppy. The second is a group of programs used for running interactive fiction. The third is a group of programs used for compression.

Zoomer

The Zoomer is a type of PDA. Zoomers all use GEOS for their OS and are / were produced by numerous different companies and are thus found under numerous different names. The "classic" Zoomers are known as the Z-7000, the Z-PDA, and the GRiDpad and were made by Casio, Tandy, and AST respectively. Newer Zoomers include HP's OmniGo models, Hyundai's Gulliver (which may not have actually been released to the general public), and Nokia's Communicator line of PDA / cell phone hybrids.

———

Made in the USA
Middletown, DE
11 August 2023

36577575R00119